Reading & Writing
Mt. Kinabalu

NATIONAL GEOGRAPHIC
L E A R N I N G

Australia • Brazil • Mexico • Singapore • United Kingdom • United States

National Geographic Learning,
a Cengage Company

Reading & Writing, Mt. Kinabalu

**Lauri Blass, Mari Vargo, Keith S. Folse,
April Muchmore-Vokoun, Elena Vestri**

Publisher: Sherrise Roehr

Executive Editor: Laura LeDréan

Managing Editor: Jennifer Monaghan

Digital Implementation Manager,
Irene Boixareu

Senior Media Researcher: Leila Hishmeh

Director of Global Marketing: Ian Martin

Regional Sales and National Account
Manager: Andrew O'Shea

Content Project Manager: Ruth Moore

Senior Designer: Lisa Trager

Manufacturing Planner: Mary Beth
Hennebury

Composition: Lumina Datamatics

For permission to use material from this text or product,
submit all requests online at **cengage.com/permissions**
Further permissions questions can be emailed to
permissionrequest@cengage.com

Student Edition: Reading & Writing, Mt. Kinabalu
ISBN-13: 978-0-357-13829-8

National Geographic Learning
20 Channel Center Street
Boston, MA 02210
USA

Locate your local office at **international.cengage.com/region**

Visit National Geographic Learning online at **ELTNGL.com**
Visit our corporate website at **www.cengage.com**

Printed in the United States of America

Print Number: 04   Print Year: 2022

PHOTO CREDITS

Scope and Sequence

Critical Thinking	Writing	Vocabulary Extension
Focus Interpreting Idiomatic Language Inferring Meaning, Synthesizing, Evaluating	**Skill Focus** Planning a Narrative Paragraph **Language for Writing** Using Time Expressions **Writing Goal** Writing a paragraph about the life of a musician or performer	**Word Link** *dis-* **Word Forms** Changing Adjectives into Nouns

Building Better Vocabulary	Original Student Writing	
Word Associations Using Collocations	**Original Student Writing** Write a narrative paragraph about an experience that you have had. **Photo Topic** Write about a surprising, frightening, happy, or funny experience you have had. **Timed Writing Topic** Write about a specific event from your childhood.	

Critical Thinking	Writing	Vocabulary Extension
Focus Inferring Attitude Applying, Synthesizing, Justifying Your Opinion	**Skill Focus** Using Pronouns to Avoid Repetition **Language for Writing** Using *And*, *But*, and *So* **Writing Goal** Writing a paragraph about a typical day in the year 2050	**Word Link** *-able* **Word Forms** Changing Verbs into Nouns

Critical Thinking		Vocabulary Extension
Focus Applying an Idea to a New Context Inferring, Synthesizing, Inferring Meaning		**Word Partners** Expressions with *challenge* **Word Partners** Expressions with *quality*

MUSIC WITH A MESSAGE

1

Musician Ta'Kaiya Blaney encourages people to care for the environment.

THINK AND DISCUSS

1 Who are some of your favorite musicians? What do you like about them?
2 In what ways do you think musicians can change the world?

BRINGING THE WORLD TOGETHER

For more than 40 years, musicians have helped bring people around the world together. For example, benefit concerts raise money and make people aware of global problems such as poverty or environmental issues.

Live 8

Live 8 was a group of benefit concerts that were held on the same day in 2005. More than a thousand musicians performed in 9 countries, including France, Japan, and South Africa. The goal was to raise money for poor countries.

Oxjam

Oxjam raises money for Oxfam, an organization that fights poverty around the world. Every October, Oxjam holds music events around the United Kingdom and Ireland. It also encourages people to hold events in their own communities.

Live Earth

The purpose of Live Earth was to help make people aware of climate change. In 2007, 150 performers appeared in concerts on every continent, including Antarctica. Audiences in over 130 countries watched the concerts on TV.

Red Rocks Amphitheatre in Colorado, U.S.A., has been the venue for some of the biggest names in world music.

Reading 1

PREPARING TO READ

BUILDING
VOCABULARY

A The words in blue below are used in the reading passage on pages 5–6. Read the paragraph. Then match the sentence parts to make definitions.

Many musicians never give up on their love for music even during difficult times. The **composer** Ludwig van Beethoven, for example, was deaf. Even though he started to lose his hearing in his 20s, Beethoven continued creating many pieces of classical music for a variety of **instruments**, such as piano and violin. Rick Allen, the drummer from Def Leppard, lost his left arm in a car accident. Although he was **disabled**, he continued to perform with a special drum set which allowed him to use his left leg to play the drums.

1. If you are a **composer**, _____   a. you can play music with.

2. An **instrument** is something _____   b. you write music.

3. If you are physically **disabled**, _____   c. you are unable to do an activity such as walking or seeing.

BUILDING
VOCABULARY

B Complete the sentences using the words in the box. Use a dictionary to help you.

> energetic   documentary   positive   appearance

1. A(n) _____ person is very active and does not feel tired easily.

2. We can describe a person's _____ with words like *short* or *pretty*.

3. Someone who is _____ believes that good things will happen.

4. A(n) _____ is a movie that gives facts and information about a topic.

USING
VOCABULARY

C Discuss these questions with a partner.

1. Which famous **composers** do you know? What do you think of their music?

2. Where in your town can you go to listen to musicians **performing** live music?

BRAINSTORMING

D Why is music important? How can music help people? Note your ideas. Then discuss with a partner.

_____

_____

PREDICTING

E Read the first paragraph of the reading passage on page 5. What do you think are some challenges disabled musicians face? Discuss with a partner. Then check your ideas as you read the passage.

_____

Staff Benda Bilili performing in London

THE POWER OF MUSIC

🎧 Track 1

A In 2004, two French filmmakers were working in Kinshasa, the capital of the Democratic Republic of the Congo (DRC). One day, they found a group of musicians performing on the streets. But these were not ordinary street musicians. Most of the band members were disabled, and they played music with homemade instruments.

THE MESSAGE IN THE MUSIC

B The band is called Staff Benda Bilili. The founders[1] of the band are Coco—the band's composer—and Ricky. Junana, the group's choreographer, designs the group's stage performances. Coude is a bass player and singer. A non-disabled member, Roger, plays the satongé—a one-string guitar. He made the instrument out of a tin can, a fish basket, and an electrical wire.

C The band's name, Staff Benda Bilili, means "look beyond appearances" in the local language. It also describes the group's mission. Staff Benda Bilili's audience was at first made up of poor street people. The band wanted to tell its audience to be positive and strong, even in difficult situations.

D "Our songs encourage kids to go to school, encourage people to work hard," says Ricky. "The message of our music is that if you want to do something with your life, you need to take things in your own hands."

[1] **founder:** a creator of something

The band members themselves are examples of their message. They don't see themselves as disabled. Instead, they see themselves as rock musicians. Their energetic performances show this. For example, when the group is playing, Junana sometimes jumps out of his wheelchair and dances around the stage on his hands.

FROM THE STREETS TO THE WORLD

The filmmakers Florent de la Tullaye and Renaud Barret were amazed by Staff Benda Bilili's music and their life stories. So they decided to make a documentary about the band. The film follows the band as it plays its music in Kinshasa, a city that had been through many wars.[2] These wars affected millions of people in Kinshasa and elsewhere in the DRC. The documentary illustrates how Staff Benda

Bilili's music helped people survive in this very difficult environment.

The film also shows the power of Staff Benda Bilili's music. The band members often wrote songs about the life problems they faced. Many of the songs offer solutions to the problems. For example, "Polio" is about living with polio[3] and getting around the city on crutches. It also tells parents the importance of vaccination for their children.

The documentary follows Staff Benda Bilili as it goes from playing in the streets of Kinshasa to playing in large European cities. Because of the film, the band became well known, and it was able to give hope to people around the world through its music.

[2] The **Second Congo War** (1998–2003) caused the deaths of as many as 5.4 million people, more than any other war since World War II.
[3] **polio:** a disease that sometimes makes people unable to use their legs

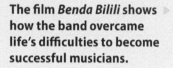

The film *Benda Bilili* shows how the band overcame life's difficulties to become successful musicians.

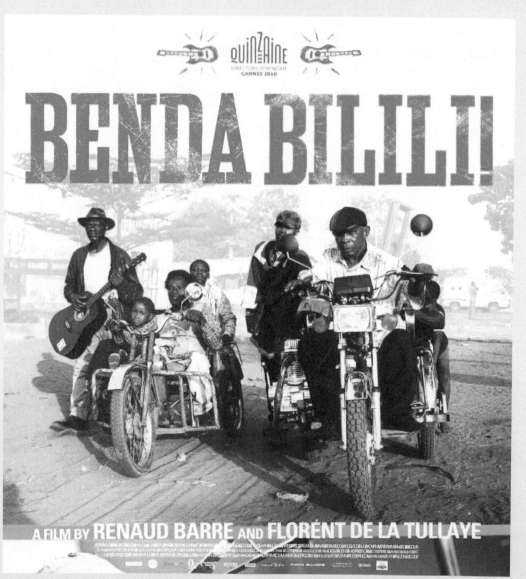

UNDERSTANDING THE READING

A What is the main idea of each section of the passage? Circle the correct answers.

UNDERSTANDING
MAIN IDEAS

1. **The Message in the Music**

   a. Staff Benda Bilili's music encourages people who live in difficult circumstances.

   b. Staff Benda Bilili encourages people to play music to deal with their problems.

2. **From the Streets to the World**

   a. Staff Benda Bilili made a film about their lives as musicians in Kinshasa.

   b. A film about Staff Benda Bilili brought the band's message to people around the world.

B Read the sentences about Staff Benda Bilili below. Circle T for *true* or F for *false.*

UNDERSTANDING
DETAILS

1. The band members made their own instruments.   T   F

2. All members of Staff Benda Bilili are disabled.   T   F

3. A satongé is a musical instrument similar to a drum.   T   F

4. At first, Staff Benda Bilili performed music for poor people.   T   F

5. The band's stage performances show how they   T   F
   overcome their disabilities.

C Find and underline the following words in the reading. Use context to identify their meanings. Then match each word to its definition (1–3).

CRITICAL THINKING:
INFERRING MEANING

choreographer (paragraph B)   **mission** (paragraph C)   **vaccination** (paragraph G)

1. _____ (n) a goal

2. _____ (n) someone who creates dances

3. _____ (n) an injection to protect against a disease

> **CRITICAL THINKING**   Writers often use **idiomatic language**—phrases that
> have a different meaning from the meaning of the actual words used. Look at the
> information around an idiomatic phrase to help you understand what it means.

D Read the sentences containing idiomatic expressions. Choose the most suitable meaning for each **bold** phrase.

CRITICAL THINKING:
INTERPRETING
IDIOMATIC
LANGUAGE

1. The band's name, Staff Benda Bilili, means "**look beyond appearances**."

   a. Judge people based on what they do and not how they look.

   b. The way people look tells you a lot about them.

2. Ricky says, "The message of our music is that . . . you need to **take things in your own hands**."

   a. It's better to fix broken things than to buy new ones.

   b. Take action on your own and don't rely on other people.

DEVELOPING READING SKILLS

READING SKILL Taking Notes

Taking notes helps you understand the main ideas of a reading passage and how supporting details relate to those ideas. It also helps you gather information for writing assignments and tests. One way to take notes is to identify main ideas and supporting details using a graphic organizer, such as a simple chart.

Abbreviations and symbols make note-taking easier and faster. You can abbreviate (shorten) words any way you want (as long as you understand your abbreviations). Some common abbreviations and symbols include:

& or + :	and	*w/* :	with	*e.g.* or *ex.* :	example
→ :	leads to/causes	= :	is/means	*b/c* :	because

TAKING NOTES **A** Complete the chart with notes from the passage on pages 5–6.

Paragraph	Main Idea / Topic	Supporting Details
B	the members of Staff Benda Bilili (SBB)	Ricky (co-founder), Junana (choreographer), Coco (co-founder & _____), Coude (bass player & singer), Roger (plays satongé)
C–D	the group's _____	- SBB = "look beyond _____" - at first, audience incl. very poor people - goal: to tell their audience to stay _____ in difficult times
E	_____ are examples of their message	- see themselves as _____ rather than disabled people - performances are very energetic
F	a _____ was made about the band	- shows SBB playing music in Kinshasa, a city that has seen many _____ - shows how SBB's music helped people survive the difficult environment
G	the power of SBB's music	- SBB writes songs about the _____ they have in their lives, e.g., one song was about living with _____
H	the impact of the film	- SBB became famous in Europe - their music gives _____ to people around the world

APPLYING **B** Choose a reading passage from an earlier unit. Create a chart like the one above to note the passage's main ideas and supporting details.

Video

American artists George Clinton and Parliament Funkadelic play at a WOMAD festival in the United Kingdom.

WORLD MUSIC

BEFORE VIEWING

A Look at the title and the caption. What do you think WOMAD stands for? Discuss with a partner.

PREDICTING

B Read the information about WOMAD. Then discuss the questions with a partner.

LEARNING ABOUT THE TOPIC

Each year, artists from around the world perform at WOMAD, an international arts festival where people can enjoy music, arts, and dance from different countries. WOMAD festivals take place in many cities around the world. The first was held in England, but since then, more than 30 countries have held their own WOMAD event.

1. What do you think WOMAD aims to do?

   _____

2. Have you been to a similar concert? What was it like?

   _____

3. How do you think WOMAD concerts might be different from other kinds of concerts, like classical or rock concerts?

   _____

   _____

VOCABULARY IN CONTEXT **C** The words in **bold** below are used in the video. Read the paragraph. Then match each word to its definition.

At WOMAD festivals, some bands play modern music like rock or rap, but others play more **traditional** music. People can also see paintings and artwork from international artists, and watch **stunning** performances by dancers. WOMAD encourages people to be **open-minded** about experiencing art and music from different countries and cultures.

1. _____ (adj) very impressive or beautiful

2. _____ (adj) existing for a long time without any change

3. _____ (adj) curious; interested to try new things

WHILE VIEWING

CATEGORIZING **A** ▶ Read the questions and watch the video. Then circle PG for *Peter Gabriel* or MC for *Marcello Colasurdo*.

1. Who co-founded WOMAD?   PG   MC

2. Who is preparing to perform at WOMAD?   PG   MC

3. Who compares his music to rap music?   PG   MC

UNDERSTANDING DETAILS **B** ▶ Watch the video again. Complete the notes about Spaccanapoli by circling the correct words.

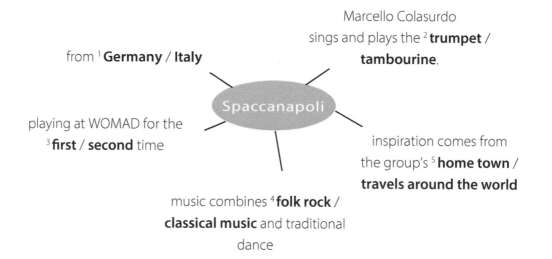

Marcello Colasurdo sings and plays the [2] **trumpet / tambourine**.

from [1] **Germany / Italy**

Spaccanapoli

playing at WOMAD for the [3] **first / second** time

inspiration comes from the group's [5] **home town / travels around the world**

music combines [4] **folk rock / classical music** and traditional dance

AFTER VIEWING

REACTING TO THE VIDEO **A** Discuss this question with a partner: If you were organizing a WOMAD event in your country, which singers or bands from your country or culture would you invite?

CRITICAL THINKING: SYNTHESIZING **B** Work with a partner. How is WOMAD similar to and different from one of the events described on page 3?

Reading 2

PREPARING TO READ

A The words in blue below are used in the reading passage on pages 12–13. Complete the sentences with the correct form of the words.

BUILDING VOCABULARY

> If you **escape** from something, you get away from it.
>
> If you **improve** something, you make it better.
>
> An **issue** is an important topic that people have different views on.
>
> A **bond** between people is a strong connection or feeling of friendship.
>
> If you **rescue** someone, you save them from something bad.
>
> A **responsibility** is a job or task you have to do.
>
> A **situation** is what is happening at a particular time.
>
> If doctors or nurses **treat** someone with an illness, they try to make them well again.

1. One global _____ that affects our planet is climate change.

2. Medical technology such as X-ray machines can help doctors identify patients' problems and _____ them effectively.

3. A firefighter's _____ is to put out fires and _____ people from burning buildings.

4. People who work together in a difficult _____ often form a strong _____.

5. Education and training can _____ the lives of people in poor countries. It can help them get jobs or start businesses, which may help them _____ a life of poverty.

B Discuss these questions with a partner: What do you think is one important social **issue** today? What are people doing to **improve** the situation?

USING VOCABULARY

_____

_____

_____

C Look at the photos and headings on pages 12–13. What kind of "change" do you think the musicians are hoping to inspire? Discuss with a partner. Then check your ideas as you read the passage.

PREDICTING

Sinikithemba means "we bring hope" in Zulu.

MUSIC FOR CHANGE

🎧 Track 2

A From ending child slavery[1] to teaching people about AIDS and world peace, musicians around the world are spreading a message of hope.

Jason Mraz: Singing for Freedom

B "If my music can contribute to happiness, then that's my main responsibility," says American singer and songwriter Jason Mraz. But Mraz does more than make people happy. He wants to use his music to make a positive change and improve people's lives.

C In 2010, Mraz visited Ghana with an organization called Free the Slaves. Its goal is to stop child slavery, a serious issue in many parts of the world. In Ghana, parents who are very poor sometimes sell their own children into slavery.

What inspired Mraz to visit Ghana? "It started with 'Freedom Song,' written by musician Luc Reynaud," he says. "I loved it, performed it, and passed it on to my friends at Free the Slaves." After seeing videos of kids in Ghana enjoying the song, he decided to visit. On **D** his trip, he worked with James Kofi Annan—a former child slave. Mraz explains that Annan works to "rescue children, and get them back to health. [He also] works with their parents to make sure they can make a living so the children aren't vulnerable[2] to traffickers."[3]

Arn Chorn-Pond: Healing with Music

E As a child, Arn Chorn-Pond worked in a prison camp in Cambodia during the Khmer Rouge period.[4] Life in the camp was terrifying.

---

[1] A **slave** is someone who is owned by other people and works for them without being paid.

[2] Someone who is **vulnerable** is weak and without protection.
[3] A **trafficker** is someone who illegally buys or sells something.

Zinhle Thabethe: Bringing Hope

National Geographic Explorer Zinhle Thabethe is a lead singer of a South African group called the Sinikithemba Choir. The members of this choir have a strong bond: They are all HIV positive. Thabethe first

G learned she had HIV in 2002. A doctor told her he could not treat her condition because medicine was not widely available. But Thabethe did not give up, and she finally found a clinic that was able to help HIV/AIDS patients.

Thabethe and other members of the Sinikithemba Choir send a message of hope to people with HIV/AIDS. She feels that she understands their situation. "I know what they

H are going through, and can help support and guide them," she says. "Only by being open and asking for help will we know that we are not alone. If you have someone who will walk the journey with you, it is always easier."

Camp workers of all ages were badly treated by the guards. Many workers died as a result. Chorn-Pond stayed alive mainly because of his skills as a musician. The camp guards liked listening to him as he played his flute.

Chorn-Pond finally escaped into the jungle, where he lived alone for many months. Later, an American aid worker met him and took him to the United States. When Chorn-Pond grew up, he went back to Cambodia. He learned that

F many traditional musicians and dancers had died during the Khmer Rouge period. So Chorn-Pond is working with older musicians to teach young Cambodians to play traditional music. In this way, he is helping a new generation keep their musical traditions alive.

[4] During the **Khmer Rouge period** (1975–1979), a political organization called Khmer Rouge governed Cambodia.

"[It is a] basic human right, to express yourself," says Chorn-Pond.

UNDERSTANDING THE READING

A Match the main ideas (1–4) to the paragraphs listed in the chart.

1. traveled overseas as part of his efforts to stop child slavery
2. is helping to keep traditional music alive
3. did not give up despite having a serious illness
4. used his musical skills to survive a dangerous period

Paragraph(s)	Main Idea	Supporting Details
C–D	Jason Mraz _____	went to _____ after seeing children enjoying "Freedom Song" worked with Annan, a former _____
E	Arn Chorn-Pond _____	played flute for _____ playing music helped C-P avoid being killed
F	Arn Chorn-Pond _____	returned to _____ as an adult works w/ _____ and teaches trad. music to _____
G	Zinhle Thabethe _____	a doctor told her that he _____ _____ she found a _____ that could help her

B Now complete the supporting details in the chart above using information from the reading passage.

C Work with a partner. Zinhle Thabethe says, "If you have someone who will walk the journey with you, it is always easier." What do you think "walk the journey" means?

_____

_____

D Look back at the reading passage. Which musician's social work do you think is most important? Why? Note your answer. Then discuss with a partner.

I think the issue of _____ is the most important because

_____

_____.

Writing

EXPLORING WRITTEN ENGLISH

A Read the sentences. Underline the words that introduce information about when an event happened.

NOTICING

1. The Live Earth event took place in 2007.
2. Thabethe first learned she had HIV in 2002.
3. Jason Mraz worked with James Kofi Annan during his visit to Ghana.
4. When Arn Chorn-Pond grew up, he went back to Cambodia.

LANGUAGE FOR WRITING Using Time Expressions

Here are a few words you can use to show when events happened in a person's life:

in + [year/phrase]   *during* + [phrase]   *when/while/after/before* + [clause]

*Yo-Yo Ma was born in Paris **in** 1955.*
*He started playing the cello **when** he was four years old.*
***After** he moved to New York, he attended the Juilliard School of Music.*
***During** his childhood, Ma performed music on TV and even played for American presidents.*

When a time phrase or clause comes first in a sentence, a comma separates it from the rest of the sentence.

***In 1998**, he started an organization. → He started an organization **in 1998**.*
***When he was four years old**, he learned to play the cello. → He learned to play the cello **when he was four years old**.*

B Complete the sentences with a time expression from the Language for Writing box. Use the information in this unit to choose the correct words. There may be more than one possible answer.

1. The first WOMAD festival was held _____ 1982.
2. Staff Benda Bilili formed _____ they were living on the streets of Kinshasa.
3. Two French filmmakers discovered Staff Benda Bilili _____ they were working in Kinshasa.
4. Staff Benda Bilili become famous around Europe _____ people saw the film about them.
5. Jason Mraz visited Ghana _____ seeing how the children loved his performance of "Freedom Song."
6. Arn Chorn-Pond worked in a prison camp in Cambodia _____ the Khmer Rouge period.
7. Chorn-Pond played music for the guards _____ he was in a prison camp.

C Make a list of three important events in your life. Then write a sentence about each one using time expressions in the Language for Writing box on page 15.

_____

_____

_____

_____

_____

_____

_____

_____

_____

WRITING SKILL Planning a Narrative Paragraph

When you write a narrative paragraph, you describe important events in the order that they happened. To plan a narrative paragraph about a person, for example, follow these steps:

Step 1 Make a timeline of events in the person's life. Include major life events such as when they were born. Also include important achievements—things that make the person interesting or admirable.

Step 2 Check your timeline. Delete unrelated or uninteresting events, but make sure you have enough events to give a clear picture of the person's life.

Step 3 Think of a topic sentence. In this case, it should be a general statement about the person that expresses what makes them special.

D Cross out three sentences that do not belong in this paragraph about Ta'Kaiya Blaney (the singer pictured on page 1).

Ta'Kaiya Blaney is a musician who is working to protect the environment and make people aware of climate change. Climate change refers to a long-term change in global weather patterns. Blaney was born in 2001 in Tla A'min Nation, an indigenous community in Canada. The community has over 1,000 people. When she was 8, she started training with a voice coach. By the time she was 10, she released her first song, _Shallow Waters_. Despite her young age, Blaney has spoken at many environmental conferences around the world. In 2011, she spoke at the TUNZA United Nations Children and Youth Conference on the Environment. Over the next three years, she was a speaker at a number of United Nations conferences in Rio de Janeiro and New York. The United Nations headquarters is in New York. Blaney was also featured in several films that raise awareness of environmental issues, such as _Saving My Tomorrow_ and _Konnected.tv_. She continues to create music that spreads positive messages. In 2015, she performed her song, _Earth Revolution_, in Paris.

E Read the paragraph about the life of the composer A.R. Rahman. Circle the event that is in the wrong order, and draw an arrow to where it should belong. Cross out one event that is not relevant.

(1) A.R. Rahman was born in Madras, India, in 1967. (2) When he was 11 years old, he dropped out of school and became a professional musician. (3) Even though he was young, he played music with some very famous Indian musicians, including Zakir Hussain. (4) After he came back to India, he started composing music for TV programs, advertisements, and later, movies. (5) Rahman received a scholarship to study music at Oxford University. (6) Oxford University is a famous university in England. (7) After Rahman got his degree, he returned to India. (8) In 2009, Rahman won an Academy Award for his music for the movie *Slumdog Millionaire*.

F Choose the most suitable topic sentence for the paragraph in exercise E.

a. A.R. Rahman is one of the world's best-known Indian musicians.

b. A.R. Rahman is known for his contributions to charity.

c. A.R. Rahman produced many famous pieces of music throughout his career.

A.R. Rahman mixes traditional music with modern electronic sounds.

WRITING TASK

GOAL You are going to write a paragraph on the following topic:

Describe the life of a musician or a performer you admire.

BRAINSTORMING **A** Think of a musician or performer that you admire. List as many events or achievements in their life as you can. Then share your ideas with a partner.

Musician / Performer	
Main life events / Key achievements	

PLANNING **B** Follow these steps to make notes for your paragraph. Don't worry about grammar or spelling. Don't write complete sentences.

Step 1 Use your notes in exercise A to make a timeline of events in this person's life. Include at least four events.

Step 2 Make sure the events are in a logical order. Do all the events help explain what you admire about the person? Delete any that are not relevant.

Step 3 Write the timeline events in the outline. Include some details about each one.

Step 4 Write a topic sentence that states what you admire about the person.

OUTLINE

Topic sentence: _____

_____

Event 1 / Details: _____

_____

Event 2 / Details: _____

_____

Event 3 / Details: _____

_____

Event 4 / Details: _____

_____

FIRST DRAFT **C** Use the information in your outline to write a first draft of your paragraph.

REVISING PRACTICE

The drafts below are similar to the one you are going to write.

What did the writer do in Draft 2 to improve the paragraph? Match the changes (a–d) to the highlighted parts.

a. improved the topic sentence
b. corrected the order of events
c. corrected a time expression
d. deleted unnecessary information

Draft 1

I admire the Chinese-American cellist Yo-Yo Ma. Ma was born in Paris, France, in 1955. He started playing the cello when he was only four years old. During he was seven, he moved with his family to New York City. He performed professionally while he was studying, and he started to become a famous cellist during that time. In New York, Ma attended the Juilliard School of Music. After that, he studied at Harvard University. In 1998, Ma founded an organization called the Silk Road Project because he wanted to use music to bring people from all over the world together. The Silk Road was an ancient road that connected Asia, the Middle East, and Europe. With the organization, Ma gives cross-cultural music performances with musicians from places like Iran, Mongolia, and Italy. Through his work, Ma is helping people all over the world appreciate different types of music.

Draft 2

I admire the Chinese-American cellist Yo-Yo Ma because he connects people around the world through music. Ma was born in Paris, France, in 1955. He started playing the cello when he was only four years old. When he was seven, he moved with his family to New York City. In New York, Ma attended the Juilliard School of Music. After that, he studied at Harvard University. He performed professionally while he was studying, and he started to become a famous cellist during that time. In 1998, Ma founded an organization called the Silk Road Project because he wanted to use music to bring people from all over the world together. With the organization, Ma gives cross-cultural music performances with musicians from places like Iran, Mongolia, and Italy. Through his work, Ma is helping people all over the world appreciate different types of music.

D Now use the questions below to revise your paragraph.

REVISED DRAFT

☐ Did you include a topic sentence about the person you are writing about?
☐ Did you put the events in order of when they happened?
☐ Do all the events relate to the person's life?
☐ Did you use time expressions correctly?

EDITING PRACTICE

Read the information below.

In sentences with time expressions, remember:
- to use *when*, *while*, *after*, and *before* at the start of a clause.
- that *during* is followed by a noun phrase, e.g., *the concert*, and not a clause.
- to use a comma when a time phrase or clause comes first in a sentence.

Correct one mistake with time expressions in each of the sentences (1–6).

1. The violinist Itzhak Perlman became famous after he performed on TV during 1958.

2. In 1998 Beyoncé's father quit his job to manage Destiny's Child.

3. Miles Davis moved to New York City to attend Juilliard, in 1945.

4. After Jay Z, heard Rihanna sing, he gave her a recording contract.

5. Lady GaGa was interested in acting before, she decided to become a singer.

6. Adele composed her first song during she was 16 years old.

FINAL DRAFT   **E**   **Follow these steps to write a final draft.**

1. Check your revised draft for mistakes with time expressions.
2. Now use the checklist on page 88 to write a final draft. Make any other necessary changes.

UNIT REVIEW

Answer the following questions.

1. Which musician/performer in this unit do you think is making the most positive impact? Why?

_____

_____

2. What does a narrative describe?

_____

_____

_____

3. Do you remember the meanings of these words? Check (✓) the ones you know. Look back at the unit and review the ones you don't know.

Reading 1:

☐ appearance   ☐ audience   ☐ composer
☐ disabled   ☐ documentary   ☐ encourage
☐ energetic AWL   ☐ instrument   ☐ perform
☐ positive AWL

Reading 2:

☐ bond AWL   ☐ escape   ☐ improve
☐ issue AWL   ☐ rescue   ☐ responsibility
☐ situation   ☐ treat

NOTES

Narrative Paragraphs

A photographer lets two trained grizzly bears nuzzle him.

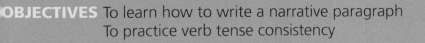

Can you write a story about something that happened in the past?

What Is a Narrative Paragraph?

A **narrative paragraph** tells a story or relates an event. Narratives have a beginning, a middle, and an end. Any time you go to a movie or read a fiction book, you are enjoying a narrative. A narrative paragraph can be fun to write because you often describe an event from your life.

A narrative paragraph:

- tells a story
- gives background information in the opening sentence or sentences
- has a clear beginning, a middle, and an end
- entertains and informs
- uses descriptive words to paint a picture so realistic that the reader can almost feel the experience of witnessing the event live

Beginning, Middle, and End

Every narrative paragraph has a beginning, a middle, and an end. Read this example paragraph from a student whose fear of public speaking causes her great grief in her speech class. Then read the explanation of the parts of the narrative paragraph that follows.

Background of story ——————▶   I never thought I could do it, but I finally conquered my fear of (topic sentence) public speaking. At the beginning of the semester, my English teacher assigned us the difficult task of speaking in front of the class for three
Beginning of story ——————▶ minutes, and I worried about it for the next two months. I have always been afraid of making a speech in public. I wrote all of my ideas on note cards. I practiced my speech with my notes in front of a mirror, in front of my cat, and in front of my husband. Would I be able to make my speech
Middle of story ——————▶ in front of my class? When the day of my speech came, I was ready. As I reached the podium, I looked at my audience and smiled. Then I looked down at my note cards. At that moment, I realized that I had the wrong information. These were the notes for my biology test, not the information about my speech! I closed my eyes and took a deep breath. Without further hesitation, I began the speech. To my surprise, the
End of story ——————▶ words flowed from my mouth. Three minutes later, it was over. Everyone applauded my speech that day, and I left that room feeling like a winner.

The Topic Sentence

    The first sentence in the paragraph—the topic sentence—gives background information about the story. The writer introduces the main character—the writer herself—and prepares her readers for the action that will come. The reader can guess from this first sentence that the story will probably be about what the writer did or what happened that made her less afraid of public speaking.

The Beginning of the Story

    The topic sentence is the beginning of the paragraph, but it is not usually the beginning of the story. The main action begins after the topic sentence. Not all narratives contain action. They may be about a problem or a conflict. In this paragraph, the writer has a problem—she has to make a speech in front of the class, but she is afraid of public speaking.

The Middle of the Story

    After the beginning part, you will find the middle part of the story. The middle part is where the main action or problem occurs. In this paragraph, that action or problem is the speech. When the writer stood in front of the class, she discovered that she had biology notes instead of speech notes.

The End of the Story

    The end of the story gives the final action or result. If there is a problem or conflict in the story, the solution is presented here. In this paragraph, the story has a happy ending. Because the writer had practiced the speech so many times, she was able to remember it without her notes. The writer learned that she had the ability to make a speech in front of a group.

Discuss the Preview Questions with your classmates. Then read the example paragraphs on pages 26–30 and answer the questions that follow.

Narrative Paragraph 1

The following paragraph is a personal story about a time when the writer was scared.

Preview Questions

1. Have you ever felt really scared? Describe the situation.

2. What was going on around you during the scary event? Give some adjectives that describe the surroundings.

3. How did the situation end?

Example Paragraph 2

My Department Store Nightmare

I will never forget the first time I got lost in New York City. I was traveling with my parents during winter vacation. We were in an incredibly large department store, and I was so excited to see such a huge place. Suddenly I turned around to ask my mom something, but she was gone! I began crying and screaming **at the top of my lungs**. A salesclerk came up to me and asked if I was OK. She got on the public address system and **notified** the customers that a little boy with blue jeans and a red cap was lost. Two minutes later, my mom and dad came running toward me. We all cried and hugged each other. This story took place over 20 years ago, but every time that I see a department store, I am reminded of that terrified little boy.

at the top of my lungs: very loudly

to notify: to give information

Post-Reading

1. What is the topic sentence of this paragraph? _____

    _____

2. Where does the story take place? _____

3. What is the beginning of the story? *(Circle one.)*

    a. He was in a large New York department store.   **b.** A salesclerk spoke to him.

4. What is the middle of the story? *(Circle one.)*

    a. He bought some jeans and a cap.   **b.** He got separated from his parents.

5. What is the end of the story? *(Circle one.)*

    a. His parents found him.   **b.** The size of the store scared him.

6. What is the writer's purpose for writing this paragraph? _____

    _____

Narrative Paragraph 2

The paragraph on the next page deals with an embarrassing moment in the writer's life.

Preview Questions

1. Think of an embarrassing moment in your life. What happened? What was the result?

2. Imagine that you are a server in a restaurant. What do you think is the most embarrassing thing that could happen to you in this job?

Talent Show <u>Disaster</u>

My most **embarrassing** moment happened during a talent show at my high school. Many other students chose to play a musical instrument, do a magic trick, or tell a joke, but I decided to sing my favorite song. I had practiced the song for many weeks and could sing it perfectly. However, this day did not go as I had planned. When my name was called, I walked on the **stage** and the curtains opened. All of a sudden, 300 people were watching me. I held the microphone in my hand, but my hands were shaking. Then the music came on. When it was time for me to sing, I forgot the song **lyrics** and missed the entire first part. Then I sang the **chorus** horribly. The **audience** tried not to laugh, but I was so embarrassed! When the song ended, I did not look at the audience and ran off the stage in **tears**.

a disaster: a complete failure

embarrassing: causing someone to feel uncomfortable

the stage: a raised area in a building or a room where people make speeches or perform

the lyrics: the words of a song

the chorus: the part of a song that repeats

the audience: a group of people who watch a show or other public event

a tear: water from your eyes when you cry

1. What is the topic sentence? _____

   _____

2. Why was the writer embarrassed? _____

   _____

   _____

3. What is the beginning of the story? (*Circle one.*)

   a. She was embarrassed.   **b.** She chose to do a song.

4. What is the middle of the story? (*Circle one.*)

   a. She could not remember the words. **b.** She wanted to change the words.

5. What is the end of the story? (*Circle one.*)

   a. She left the room quickly.   **b.** She helped some of the audience.

6. What is the writer's purpose for writing this story? _____

   _____

   _____

Narrative Paragraph 3

The example narrative on the next page tells about a time in a boy's life when he was unhappy. He learned an important lesson from his unhappiness.

Preview Questions

1. Think of your best friend. How long have you been best friends?

2. What are the most important qualities in a friend?

3. Have you ever moved away and had to make new friends? Describe the situation. Was it easy? If not, how did you overcome this situation?

A Lesson in Friendship

I learned the hard way how to make friends in a new school. At my old school in Toronto, I was on the football and track teams, so I was very popular and had lots of friends. Everything changed when I was 16 years old because my parents decided to move to Florida. Going to a new school was not easy for me. The first few days in my new school were extremely difficult. The class schedule was different, and the teachers were more informal than in my old school. All the students dressed **casually** in shorts and T-shirts instead of a school uniform. Some kids tried to be nice to me, but I did not want to talk to them. To me, they looked and acted **funny**! After a few weeks, I realized that no one even tried to talk to me anymore. I began to feel lonely. Two months passed before I got the courage to talk to a few classmates. Finally, I realized that they were normal people, just like me. I began to develop some **relationships** and eventually some good friendships. I learned a **valuable** lesson about making friends that year.

casually: informally

funny: strange

a relationship: a friendship
valuable: important

Post-Reading

1. What is the general topic of this paragraph? _____
   _____

2. What is the topic sentence? _____
   _____

3. In your own words, what is the beginning of the story?
   _____
   _____
   _____
   _____

4. In your own words, what is the middle of the story?
   _____
   _____
   _____
   _____

5. In your own words, what is the end of the story?
   _____
   _____
   _____
   _____

6. What lesson did the writer learn from this experience?
   _____
   _____
   _____
   _____

Working with Ideas for Narrative Paragraphs

You can find stories from your own memories and experiences. Many times, the best narrative stories are about real events that actually happened to someone. In fact, there is an expression in English that "truth is stranger than fiction," which means that it is sometimes more difficult to invent a story ("fiction") than to tell about something that actually happened ("truth").

ACTIVITY 2 **Recognizing Good Topics for Narrative Paragraphs**

Read the following paragraph titles. Put a check (✓) next to the titles that you think would make good narrative paragraphs. Be prepared to explain your choices.

_____ My Best Friend, Luke   _____ Natural Disasters

_____ How to Become a Doctor   _____ Bears

_____ The Day I Almost Died   _____ A Wonderful Day in the Mountains

Compare your choices with a classmate. Do you agree on which titles would make the best narrative paragraphs? Explain why or why not.

Using Descriptive Language to Help Readers See Your Story

In narrative writing, you want the readers to be able to imagine that they are actually in the story with you. In order to accomplish this goal, you need to describe your story and your experiences as carefully as possible. Use specific vocabulary to help your readers imagine that they are actually there with you in your story. Your goal is to make your readers understand why this event is so special or significant for you.

Sentence	General Vocabulary	More Descriptive Vocabulary
The movie was _____.	nice	interesting, thrilling, inspiring, heart-warming, superb
These essays are _____.	bad	boring, horrible, empty, dull, shocking, violent
I felt _____.	good	marvelous, fantastic, elated, wonderful, relaxed
We were _____.	afraid	terrified, anxious, alarmed, scared, petrified

Describing a Moment

Think about a moment in your life where something interesting or unusual happened, or look at the photograph for ideas. What was happening before that moment, during that moment, and right after that moment? Write some details about that moment, including the place, things that happened, your feelings, and how you feel today. Use descriptive language.

Moment: _____

Where were you? _____

What happened?   Before: _____

_____

During: _____

_____

After: _____

_____

What were you feeling?   Before: _____

_____

During: _____

_____

After: _____

_____

Your overall impression or feeling: _____

33

ACTIVITY 4 **Sequencing Sentences in a Paragraph**

These sentences form a narrative of a personal experience with death. Read the sentences and number them from 1 to 7 to indicate the best order.

_____ **a.** At 7:18 the next morning, a severe earthquake measuring 8.1 on the Richter scale hit Mexico City. I was asleep, but the violent side-to-side movement of my bed woke me up. Then I could hear the rumble of the building as it was shaking.

_____ **b.** As I was trying to stand up, I could hear the walls of the building cracking. I was on the third floor of a six-story building, and I thought the building was going to collapse. I really believed that I was going to die.

_____ **c.** I flew to Mexico City on September 17. The first two days were uneventful.

_____ **d.** My trip to Mexico City in September 1985 was not my first visit there, but this unforgettable trip helped me realize something about life.

_____ **e.** I visited a few friends and did a little sightseeing. On the evening of the eighteenth, I had a late dinner with some friends that I had not seen in several years. After a very peaceful evening, I returned to my hotel and quickly fell asleep.

_____ **f.** In the end, approximately 5,000 people died in this terrible tragedy, but I was lucky enough not to be among them. This unexpected disaster taught me that life can be over at any minute, so it is important for us to live every day as if it is our last.

_____ **g.** When I looked at my room, I could see that the floor was moving up and down like water in the ocean. Because the doorway is often the strongest part of a building, I tried to stand up in the doorway of the bathroom.

ACTIVITY 5 Copying a Paragraph

Now copy the sentences from Activity 4 in the best order for a narrative paragraph. Add a title of your choice.

Example Paragraph 5

Title _____

*Background
information
(topic sentence)* _____

_____

_____

Beginning of story _____

_____

_____

_____

Middle of story _____

_____

_____

_____

_____

_____

_____

End of story _____

_____

_____

_____

_____

Grammar for Writing

Maintaining Verb Tense Consistency

When writers tell a story, they usually use the simple past tense and perhaps the past progressive tense. Be careful to keep the verb tense consistent, or the same. For example, if your story begins with the simple past tense, do not suddenly switch to the simple present tense and then go back to the simple past tense.

Explanation	Examples
Use the **present tense** to show a general truth or activity.	My friends **live** in Mexico.
Use the **present progressive tense** to show an action that is in progress at this moment.	My friends **are living** in Mexico now.
Use the **simple past tense** to show that something happened in the past.	My friends **lived** in Mexico in 1985.
Use the **past progressive tense** to show that something was in progress at a specific time.	My friends **were living** in Mexico when the earthquake happened.

ACTIVITY 6 Identifying Verb Tenses

Read this narrative paragraph. Circle the verbs. The verbs in the first two sentences have been done for you. Then answer the questions that follow.

Example Paragraph 6

Ali's Surprise

Ali (knew) how difficult it (was) to get a student visa for the United States. However, he (gathered) all the important paperwork, including his I–20 document, passport, bank statements, and even a letter from his doctor. On the cold morning of his interview, he jumped on a bus to the capital. For five long hours, he rode in silence, looked out the window at the gray landscape, and wondered about the interview. When he arrived at the embassy, he saw a line of more than 100 people. He patiently waited until a guard gave him a number to enter the warm building. The faces of the embassy personnel frightened him, except for an older woman who reminded him of his grandmother. She was working at window number 4. He hoped that she would be the one to look at his paperwork. When it was his turn, he looked up quickly. A baby-faced worker at window number 3 was calling him to

come up. Ali stepped up to the window and gave all his documents to the young embassy employee. He glanced at "Grandma" and thought his chance was gone. Then he heard her message to another man, "You will not get a visa in a thousand years! Next in line, please." Ali was shocked. He turned to the embassy worker in front of him. The worker said, "Here you are, sir. Your student visa is valid for one year." Ali could not believe it. The impossible had happened. Happily, he took his passport and left the building.

1. What tense is used for most of the verbs in this paragraph? _____

2. A few of the verbs are not in this tense. Can you explain this ? _____

_____

_____

_____

_____

ACTIVITY 7 **Using Correct Verb Tenses**

Read the following narrative paragraph. Circle all the verbs. Then make corrections so that all the verbs are in a tense that expresses past time—either the simple past tense or the past progressive tense.

Example Paragraph 7

My First Job

The happiest day of my life is when I get my first job last year. After college, I try and try for six months to get a job with an advertising firm, but my luck is bad. Finally, one day while I am eating a sandwich in a downtown coffee shop, my luck will begin to change. A young woman who is sitting next to me asks if she could read my newspaper. I say OK, and we start talking. She begins to tell me that she is an executive in a huge advertising company and is looking for an assistant. I will tell her that I am very interested in mass communications and study it for four years at the university. She gives me her business card, and within one week, I am her administrative assistant. It is the best lunch of my life!

Read the teacher's four comments below and the four narrative paragraphs on pages 40–43. Match each teacher comment to the correction needed in each paragraph. Write the number on the line at the end of the paragraph.

Teacher Comments

1. *Your first sentence is too specific to be a topic sentence. Who is "her"? Your topic sentence should tell the reader what the paragraph is going to be about.*

2. *Be careful with verbs. The verbs you used jump from the simple present to the simple past tense.*

3. *Your paragraph is good. However, you didn't indent the first line of your paragraph. Be careful with correct paragraph form.*

4. *This isn't a narrative paragraph—it is a descriptive one. Follow directions more carefully.*

A Problem with My Creation

I took pottery lessons with her for many years, but this one time her advice led to a disaster. I made a **vase** from clay that weighed about five pounds. The clay was very wet when I finished, and it needed to dry before I could put the vase in the oven. I asked her how long I had to wait, and she told me about one week. Because it was my first time making such a large vase, I did **not think twice about** her advice. However, one week later, my vase was still wet. She put it in the oven anyway. Not long after, we heard a loud popping noise. It scared both of us, and we ran to the oven to see what was wrong. When she finally opened the oven, pieces of clay were everywhere. Because there were too many air bubbles in the wet clay, my vase exploded. It was the most terrible incident ever! After we cleaned up the mess, my pottery teacher **apologized** and said she would help me make another vase.

a vase: a container for flowers and water

to not think twice about something: do something without thinking

to apologize: say you are sorry

Teacher Comment: _____

My Favorite Place

My bedroom is small but comfortable. The walls are covered with posters and banners of my favorite sports teams. On the left side, there is a small bed that I have had since I was ten years old. Next to the bed is my dresser. It is blue and white with gold **knobs**. Beside the dresser is my bookshelf, which holds most of my schoolbooks, dictionaries, and novels. Across from the bookshelf, you can see my closet. It is too small to hold all my clothes, so I hang some of my stuff on my chair. The clothes get **wrinkled** there, but I do not mind. My mom does not like it that my room is so messy, so one of these days I am going to clean it up and make her happy.

a knob: a small round handle on a drawer or door

wrinkled: not smooth, with lines

Teacher Comment: _____

A Travel Nightmare

When I decided to travel across Europe with a backpack, I did not think I would meet the local police. My best friend and I were sitting in Frankfurt on a train bound for Paris when the nightmare began. A young man comes to the window of the train and asks me what time the train leaves. It took us only ten seconds to open the window and answer him. When we turned away from the window and sat down in our seats, we noticed that our backpacks were missing. Quickly, we got off the train and went to the police headquarters inside the station. We explained what happened. The police officers did not look surprised. They say it is a common way of stealing bags. One person stays outside the train and asks a passenger for help or information. While the passenger is talking to this person, someone else comes quietly into the train car and steals bags, purses, or other valuables. The team players are so good at it that they can steal what they want in less than three seconds. The police officers tell us that there is really nothing we can do, but they suggest that we look through the garbage cans and hope that the robbers took only our money and threw our passports and bags away. We look and look but we never found our bags. The next morning, we are not in Paris; we are at our embassy in Frankfurt, waiting for new passports.

Teacher Comment: _____

The Trick That Failed

Twin brothers Freddie and Felix often played tricks at school, but one day they went too far. On that day they decided to try to cheat on a French exam. Freddie was very good at learning languages and was always the best student in both Spanish and French. Felix, however, excelled in mathematics. He was not interested in languages at all. When Felix discovered that he had to take a standardized exam in French, he asked his brother for help. The day of Felix's test, they met in the boys' restroom during lunch and switched clothes. Freddie went to his brother's French class and took the test for him. Meanwhile, Felix followed Freddie's schedule. After school, the twins laughed about their trick and headed home. As they entered the house, their mother called them into the kitchen. She was furious! She had received a phone call from the school principal. The French teacher had found out about the trick! "How did he know?" cried Felix. "Easily," replied his mother. "Everyone at the school knows that one obvious difference between you and your brother is that you are right-handed and Freddie is left-handed. While the French teacher was grading the tests, he noticed that the check marks on the test were

made by a left-handed person." Felix and Freddie got into a lot of trouble that day, but they learned a valuable lesson—and they never cheated again.

Teacher Comment: _____

Building Better Vocabulary

ACTIVITY 9 Word Associations

Circle the word or phrase that is most closely related to the word or phrase on the left. If necessary, use a dictionary to check the meaning of words you do not know.

	A	B
1. heart-warming	a bad feeling	a good feeling
2. valuable	important	not important
3. grief	negative	positive
4. a rumble	a noise	a smell
5. to flow	to move	to seem
6. applauded	negative	positive
7. came up to me	approached me	persuaded me
8. to switch	to appreciate	to change
9. class is over at 9	it begins at 9	it ends at 9
10. to witness	to see	to think
11. to collapse	to cancel	to fall
12. scary	afraid	necessary
13. casually	formal	not formal
14. a tragedy	a bad event	a good event
15. to hug	to embrace	to prosper

Fill in each blank with the word on the left that most naturally completes the phrase on the right. If necessary, use a dictionary to check the meaning of words you do not know.

1. chance / task   a difficult _____

2. at / up   to set _____

3. deep / hard   to take a _____ breath

4. lesson / nightmare   a valuable _____

5. of / on   What's going _____ ?

6. hear / see   _____ the rumble

7. natural / tense   a _____ disaster

8. shirt / truck   a wrinkled _____

9. ears / lungs   screamed at the top of her _____

10. against / without   _____ any hesitation at all

Original Writing Practice: Narrative Paragraph

ACTIVITY 11 **Original Writing Practice**

Write a narrative paragraph about an experience that you have had. Follow these guidelines:

- Choose a topic such as your first time driving a car, your graduation day, or a special event in your life.
- Brainstorm the events in your story.
- Write a topic sentence with controlling ideas.
- Give enough background information to help your readers understand the setting.
- Write supporting sentences for the middle of your narrative.
- Check for consistency in simple past and past progressive verbs.
- Use descriptive vocabulary words.
- Write the end of the story.
- Use at least two of the vocabulary words or phrases presented in Activity 9 and Activity 10. Underline these words and phrases in your paragraph.

If you need ideas for words and phrases, see the Useful Vocabulary for Better Writing on pages 118–122.

ACTIVITY 12 Peer Editing

Exchange papers from Activity 11 with a partner. Read your partner's paragraph. Then use Peer Editing Sheet 1 on ELTNGL.com/sites/els to help you comment on your partner's paragraph. Be sure to offer positive suggestions and comments that will help your partner improve his or her writing. Consider your partner's comments as you revise your own paragraph.

Additional Topics for Writing

Here are some ideas for narrative paragraphs. When you write your paragraph, follow the guidelines in Activity 11.

PHOTO
TOPIC: Look at the photo on pages 22–23. Write about a surprising, frightening, happy, or funny experience you have had.

TOPIC 2: Create a short story using an animal as the main character. What happens to this animal? You can tell a story from your own country or culture that you think foreigners would not know.

TOPIC 3: Write about how someone you know got in trouble. What happened?

TOPIC 4: Write about an important lesson that you have learned from a real experience.

TOPIC 5: Write about the most memorable movie you have seen. Briefly explain the plot (story) of the film.

Timed Writing

How quickly can you write in English? There are many times when you must write quickly, such as on a test. It is important to feel comfortable during those times. Timed-writing practice can make you feel better about writing quickly in English.

1. Take out a piece of paper.

2. Read the writing prompt.

3. Brainstorm ideas for five minutes.

4. Write a short narrative paragraph (six to ten sentences).

5. You have 25 minutes to write.

Choose a specific event from your childhood that you consider special or significant. Why do you still remember this event? You might decide to write about your first day of school, a particularly difficult class or exam, a time when you were called to the principal's office for something you had done, or one of your early birthday parties. Describe the people and places that are related to the event. Use descriptive language to help your readers imagine that they were actually there with you at the event. Your goal is to make your readers clearly understand why this event is so special or significant to you.

NOTES

FUTURE LIVING

3

A robot named I-FAIRY
conducts a wedding in Tokyo.

ACADEMIC SKILLS

READING	Identifying examples
WRITING	Using pronouns to avoid repetition
GRAMMAR	Using *and*, *but*, and *so*
CRITICAL THINKING	Inferring attitude

THINK AND DISCUSS

1 How do you think life will be different 50 years from now? How about in 100 years?
2 Do you think we will live on other planets someday? Why or why not?

A Look at the information on these pages and answer the questions.

1. Which future technology or feature do you think is most useful?

2. Are any of these happening already? Can you give an example?

B Match the words in blue to their definitions.

_____ (v) to change in order to deal with something

_____ (n) scientific knowledge or skill

_____ (v) to say what will happen in the future

THE CITY OF THE FUTURE

What will cities be like in the future? Experts predict that technology will change the design of our cities and the way we live.

Wearable technology

People will wear devices that communicate with their surroundings. The devices will provide useful information as they move around the city.

Underground travel

More people will ride bicycles and other forms of travel that don't pollute the environment. In busy areas, they will ride underground in special bicycle lanes to avoid traffic.

Solar power

Most homes and apartment buildings will generate their own power with solar panels. They will also share this electricity with the rest of the city.

Car technology

Most people will have driverless cars. Cars will communicate with each other. They will tell each other where to go to avoid traffic.

Personalized advertising

Advertisements on signs will **adapt** to whoever is walking by. The signs will recognize the person and show them ads for products they might be interested in.

Reading 1

PREPARING TO READ

BUILDING
VOCABULARY **A** The words in blue below are used in the reading passage on pages 51–52. Read the sentences. Then match the correct form of each word to its definition.

> Most companies have their own computer **networks**. These networks **link** computers to each other.
>
> Pepper is a **sociable** robot that's able to understand people's feelings and change the way it communicates with them.
>
> You can **store** information like phone numbers and addresses on your smartphone.
>
> Online movie and TV sites **suggest** films and shows based on your **preferences** and what you usually watch.
>
> Driverless cars are an example of **intelligent** technology. They can take you where you want to go, avoid traffic, and park themselves.

1. _____ (v) to connect

2. _____ (adj) friendly to people

3. _____ (n) what you like or don't like

4. _____ (v) to give people ideas about what they should do

5. _____ (adj) able to understand and learn things

6. _____ (n) a system of connected communication lines

7. _____ (v) to keep somewhere for future use

USING
VOCABULARY **B** Discuss these questions with a partner: What are some examples of **intelligent** devices you know or use? What can they do?

BRAINSTORMING **C** List some technologies that make life easier or more fun today than in the past.

Technologies That Make Life Easier	Technologies That Make Life More Fun
high-speed trains	3-D movies

PREDICTING **D** Skim the reading passage on pages 51–52 quickly. Check (✓) the topics that the passage covers. Then check your answers as you read.

☐ 1. cars that drive themselves   ☐ 3. computers that control the house

☐ 2. things in the home that send   ☐ 4. robots that are like people
     information to one another

In the future, new technology will change many of our daily routines.

HOW WILL WE LIVE?

Track 3

A Picture this: You wake up in the morning. A soft light turns on in your room. You go into the bathroom and the shower starts. The water is the perfect temperature. After your shower, you go into the kitchen. Your favorite breakfast is already cooked, and it's on the table, ready to eat. Now it's time to go to work. It's a rainy day. You live alone, but you find that your umbrella and hat are already by the door. How is all this possible? Welcome to your future life!

APPLIANCES THAT TALK

B Technology will allow homes in the future to be "smart." Appliances will communicate with each other—and with you. Your stove, for instance, will tell you when your food is cooked and ready to eat. Refrigerators will suggest recipes based on food items you already have.

C The technology is possible because of tiny information-storing devices called RFID[1] chips. People already use them to keep track of pets and farm animals. Future RFID chips will store information about all the items in your cabinets.[2] For example, they will record the date that you bought each item. Other devices will "read" this information using radio waves. When you need more food, your cabinets will tell you to buy it.

[1] **RFID** stands for "radio-frequency identification."
[2] A **cabinet** is a type of cupboard used for storing medicine, drinks, and other items.

HOUSES THAT THINK

D   Are you tired of the color or pattern of your walls? In a smart home, you won't have to repaint them. The walls will actually be digital screens, like computer or TV screens. The technology is called OLED,[3] and it's here already. OLEDs are tiny devices that use electricity to light things. You can find the same technology in today's thin TV screens. OLED walls can become clear, like windows, or display colors and patterns, like walls.

E   A computer network will link these walls with everything else in your house. This intelligent technology works like a computer "brain" that controls your entire house. It will also adapt to your preferences. Your house can learn about your likes and dislikes. It will then use that knowledge to control the environment. For example, it will set the heat in the house to your favorite temperature. It will turn on the shower at the right heat. It will also darken the windows at night and lighten them when it's time to wake up.

ROBOTS THAT FEEL?

F   But how about your cooked breakfast, and the umbrella and hat you found by the door? For those, you can thank your robot helper. Futurologists predict that many homes will have robots in the future. Robots already do many things, such as building cars and vacuuming floors. But scientists today are starting to build friendlier, more intelligent robots—ones that people will feel more comfortable having around in the house.

G   Sociable robots will be able to show feelings with their faces, just like humans. They will smile and frown, make eye contact, and speak. These robots will do work around the house, such as cooking and cleaning. They will even take care of children and the elderly.

H   How soon will this smart home be a reality? There's a good chance it will be a part of your life in the next 10 years, perhaps sooner. Much of the technology is already here.

[3]**OLED** stands for "organic light-emitting diode."

Robots like **ASIMO** can already do many things that people do.

UNDERSTANDING THE READING

A Match each main idea below to a paragraph (A–H) from the reading. Three paragraphs are extra.

UNDERSTANDING
MAIN IDEAS

     _____ 1. An intelligent electronic system will control an entire house.

     _____ 2. Information-storing technology will allow parts of the house to communicate with us.

     _____ 3. Digital technology will allow us to change the design of our homes.

     _____ 4. Intelligent homes may be a part of our everyday life within 10 years.

     _____ 5. Robots that act like humans will do housework and take care of people.

B According to the passage, is each statement below true? Or is it not mentioned? Circle T for *true*, F for *false*, or NG for *not given*.

UNDERSTANDING
DETAILS

Appliances That Talk

1. Appliances will make personalized suggestions using information they collect.   **T F NG**

2. RFID is a type of smart refrigerator that can recommend recipes.   **T F NG**

Houses That Think

3. Future technology will make houses safer from natural disasters.   **T F NG**

4. Houses will be able to change the temperature of the room based on your preferences.   **T F NG**

Robots That Feel?

5. Robots will have human-like expressions.   **T F NG**

6. Sociable robots will help us in our homes.   **T F NG**

> **CRITICAL THINKING** **Inferring** a writer's **attitude** means thinking about how they feel about the subject. Ask yourself: Is the author generally positive or negative? What clues indicate the author's attitude?

C Work with a partner. First, circle a word to complete the sentence below. Then find an example from the passage that supports your answer.

CRITICAL THINKING:
INFERRING
ATTITUDE

The author of the reading passage seems **positive / negative** about life in the future.

According to the author, _____

_____

_____

D Discuss these questions with a partner.

CRITICAL THINKING:
APPLYING

1. Which future technologies in the reading would you like to have in your home?

2. Can you think of any other household technologies that would be useful?

DEVELOPING READING SKILLS

> **READING SKILL** Identifying Examples
>
> Writers often give examples to support their ideas. Here are some common words or phrases they use. Note the position of the commas.
>
> *Someday, your refrigerator will be able to communicate with you.* **For example**, *it will suggest recipes based on food you already have.*
>
> *People use RFID chips today for many things,* **such as** *keeping track of pets and farm animals.*
>
> *In the future, robots will be more like humans.* **For instance**, *they will smile, frown, make eye contact, and speak.*

IDENTIFYING
EXAMPLES

A Circle the words and phrases that introduce examples in the following paragraph about Wakamaru. Then underline the examples.

Engineers in Japan built a sociable robot named Wakamaru. They designed Wakamaru to help and serve people in a friendly, caring, and intelligent way. For instance, Wakamaru can recognize faces, use gestures, and understand 10,000 Japanese words. It is able to talk to people about a variety of topics, such as the weather and the news. Wakamaru can do many tasks for a family. For example, at night, it moves quietly around the house, but it can wake family members up if there is any trouble. During the day, Wakamaru can send them email and text messages.

IDENTIFYING
EXAMPLES

B Match each example (a–e) to a sentence or sentence part (1–5).

_____ 1. Mobile technology has changed the way we shop.

_____ 2. I think intelligent robots can help with dangerous tasks,

_____ 3. Everyday activities,

_____ 4. Some people are worried about the safety of using smart technology.

_____ 5. There are many ways we can reduce the number of cars on the road.

a. such as looking for people after a natural disaster.

b. Hackers, for instance, could steal personal information stored on our phones.

c. For example, we could cycle to work instead of driving.

d. such as cleaning and cooking, could be made more convenient with intelligent technology.

e. For example, we can buy things through an app on our smartphone.

INTRODUCING
EXAMPLES

C Add an example or examples to each sentence. Use a suitable phrase to introduce the example(s).

1. I think living in a smart home would make life more convenient. _____

   _____

2. I would like to live with a robot. I would ask it to do many things, _____

   _____

Video

NASA's Curiosity Rover explores Mars to help scientists study the planet.

LIVING ON MARS

BEFORE VIEWING

A Look at the photo and the title of the video. What do you think are some of the challenges of living on Mars? Discuss with a partner.

PREDICTING

B Read the information about Mars. Then note the three reasons why Mars may be a suitable planet for people to live on.

LEARNING ABOUT THE TOPIC

Of all the planets near Earth, Mars is the best possible option for humans to live on. There are many reasons why Mars is our first choice. First of all, the length of a day on Mars is more similar to the length of a day on Earth than any other planet in our solar system. A day on Mars lasts about 24 hours, but a day on Venus lasts about 243 Earth days. In addition, Mars gets enough light from the sun. This means we can use solar panels for power. Finally, even though Mars is much colder than Earth, its temperature is closer than other planets to Earth's temperature. Venus, for instance, is much too hot—its average temperature is over 400 degrees Celsius.

1. _____

2. _____

3. _____

C The words in **bold** below are used in the video. Read the paragraph. Then match the correct form of each word to its definition.

There have been dozens of **missions** to Mars during the past 30 years, but no humans have ever gone there. Some scientists have **ambitious** plans to **colonize** Mars. However, we have to make changes to Mars's **atmosphere** before we can live there. For example, we need to make it warmer, and we have to add oxygen (O_2) into the air.

1. _____ (n) the air space above a planet

2. _____ (v) to go to a place, live in it, and control it

3. _____ (n) an important job that usually involves travel

4. _____ (adj) very difficult or challenging to do

WHILE VIEWING

A ▶ Watch the video. Circle the name of the correct scientist.

1. **Dr. McKay** / **Dr. Zubrin** is disappointed that humans haven't been to Mars yet.
2. **Dr. McKay** / **Dr. Zubrin** is doing research to prepare for a mission to Mars.
3. **Dr. McKay** / **Dr. Zubrin** studies how we can change the atmosphere on Mars.

B ▶ Watch the video again. Why do the scientists say we will be successful in colonizing Mars? Check (✓) the reasons mentioned in the video.

☐ 1. Countries around the world are now working together on a mission to Mars.

☐ 2. We are doing research in places that have similar conditions to Mars.

☐ 3. We have successfully grown a plant on Mars.

☐ 4. We know how to warm the atmosphere on Mars.

☐ 5. We know a way to create oxygen on Mars.

AFTER VIEWING

A Discuss with a partner: Do you think it's a good idea for people to go to Mars? Why or why not?

☐ Yes, I do.   ☐ I'm not sure.   ☐ Definitely not.

Reason:

_____

B Which technologies in the reading on pages 51–52 might be useful for living on Mars? Why? Note your ideas and discuss with a partner.

_____

_____

_____

Reading 2

PREPARING TO READ

A The words in blue below are used in the reading passage on pages 58–59. Read the paragraph. Then match the correct form of each word to its definition.

BUILDING VOCABULARY

We know that it is very cold on Mars. Scientists recorded the temperature in several places on the planet. They took these temperatures to find out the **average** temperature on Mars, which is minus 60 degrees Celsius. Because the temperature is so low, there is no **liquid** on Mars—only ice. Carbon dioxide (CO_2) is **trapped** in this ice—it cannot get out. However, heat can melt the ice and turn it into water. This can **release** the carbon dioxide into the atmosphere. When the **level** of carbon dioxide increases in the atmosphere, Mars will become warmer.

1. _____ (v) to stop holding; to let go

2. _____ (adj) the middle of two extremes

3. _____ (v) to hold and keep from moving

4. _____ (n) a substance that flows freely, such as water or oil

5. _____ (n) a point on a scale, usually showing the amount of something

B Complete the sentences below using the words in the box. Use your dictionary to help you with the meanings of the words.

BUILDING VOCABULARY

environment   plants   lack

1. _____ need sun and water to grow.

2. Earth's _____ is very suitable for life.

3. The _____ of oxygen on high mountains makes it difficult to breathe.

C Discuss these questions with a partner.

USING VOCABULARY

1. What kind of **plants** grow well in your area?
2. What kind of **environment** is best for growing plants?

D Read the title of the reading passage and look at the picture on pages 58–59. What do you think the passage is about? Then check your answer as you read.

PREDICTING

a. the technology we will use to travel to Mars and other planets

b. what an average day on Mars will be like for people in the future

c. how we can make Mars a place where people can live

AT HOME ON MARS

A Will humans someday live and work on Mars? Many scientists think so. In fact, they are already working on plans to turn Mars into a new Earth.

B Humans need three basic things to live: water to drink, air to breathe, and food to eat. Because of the lack of these necessities, it isn't possible to live on Mars right now. For one thing, there is not enough oxygen. There is also no liquid water—just some ice. So how can we make Mars habitable?[1] The answer, scientists suggest, is a process called *terraforming*.

C Terraforming means changing the environment of a planet so that it is similar to Earth's. On Mars, the average temperature is about minus 60 degrees Celsius. So one goal of terraforming Mars is to warm it up. Most scientists agree that Earth is becoming warmer due to increased levels of greenhouse gases in our atmosphere. We might be able to create similar conditions on Mars.

D One solution is to build factories on Mars that release greenhouse gases. The gases will change the Martian atmosphere, resulting in warmer temperatures. Mars's polar regions will begin to melt, releasing more carbon dioxide trapped inside the ice. Rain will eventually fall. It may then be possible to grow plants outdoors for food. The plants will add oxygen to the air, making human colonies on Mars a real possibility.

[1] If a place is **habitable**, you can live there.

TURNING THE RED PLANET GREEN

1 FIRST VISITS

E Terraforming Mars will probably be a thousand-year project, starting with several survey missions. The flight to Mars will take 6 months, but the entire mission might last more than 18 months.

2 HOMES ON MARS

F Each new mission will build more habitation modules—places to live. These will allow future visitors to spend more time on Mars and learn more about living on the planet.

3 GLOBAL WARMING

G Factories on Mars will release carbon dioxide into the atmosphere, warming the planet and allowing water to flow.

4 LIFE UNDER DOMES

H Enormous domes will provide climate-controlled living spaces, first for plants and later for humans. It will take centuries to improve the rocky surface so that people can grow plants.

5 POWERING THE PLANET

I Nuclear power[2] and wind turbines[3] are two current technologies that we might be able to use on Mars.

6 DON'T FORGET YOUR MASK

J Even 1,000 years from now, there may not be enough oxygen for humans to breathe, so people on Mars may still need to use special breathing equipment.

[2]**Nuclear power** comes from the energy that is released when the central parts of atoms are split or combined.
[3]**Wind turbines** are engines with blades. They produce power when wind spins the blades.

UNDERSTANDING THE READING

UNDERSTANDING
MAIN IDEAS

A Read the first sentence of a summary of paragraphs A–D. Check (✓) three other sentences to complete the summary.

If we want to live on Mars someday, we will have to change it so it is similar to Earth.

- ☐ 1. Wind turbines can produce power using wind energy.
- ☐ 2. We will need to increase the average temperature of Mars.
- ☐ 3. A huge amount of greenhouse gases is making Earth's atmosphere warmer.
- ☐ 4. Releasing greenhouse gases on Mars will help create a suitable environment.
- ☐ 5. Changing Mars will be a long process, but scientists think we will live there someday.

SEQUENCING

B How do scientists plan to terraform Mars? Use information from pages 58–59 to complete the timeline.

- a. Factories on Mars's surface produce carbon dioxide.
- b. Rain begins to fall and water flows.
- c. Early visitors build living spaces.
- d. Plants can grow on Mars's surface.
- e. The temperature on Mars begins to rise.
- f. Ice in polar regions starts to melt.

first survey
mission

humans
colonize Mars

IDENTIFYING
PROBLEMS AND
SOLUTIONS

C Write a short answer to each question.

1. How might human visitors get their power on Mars?

_____

_____

2. What will still be a problem for humans on Mars 1,000 years from now?

_____

_____

CRITICAL THINKING:
JUSTIFYING
YOUR OPINION

D Some companies are planning a trip to Mars and are looking for people to join them. Would you join a mission to Mars? Check your answer below. Then write two sentences to explain your reasons.

☐ Yes, I'd love to.   ☐ I'm not sure.   ☐ Definitely not.

Reasons:

1._____

2._____

Writing

EXPLORING WRITTEN ENGLISH

A Read the sentences below. Check (✓) the ones where the underlined part is ...

NOTICING

1. **an additional idea:**

☐ a. Humans need three basic things to live: water to drink, air to breathe, and <u>food to eat</u>.

☐ b. There will be <u>many difficulties in terraforming Mars</u>.

2. **a contrasting idea:**

☐ a. A computer network will link these walls with <u>everything else in your house</u>.

☐ b. Robots already do many things such as building cars and vacuuming floors. But <u>scientists today are starting to build friendlier, more intelligent robots</u>.

3. **a result:**

☐ a. Some scientists believe that <u>it's possible to colonize Mars in the future</u>.

☐ b. Even 1,000 years from now, there may still not be enough oxygen for humans to breathe, so <u>people on Mars may still need to use special breathing equipment</u>.

LANGUAGE FOR WRITING Using *And*, *But*, and *So*

You can use the conjunctions *and*, *but*, and *so* to connect information in sentences.

And introduces an additional idea ...

• to connect words: *People will visit <u>Mars</u> **and** <u>Venus</u>.*

• to connect phrases: *People will <u>visit Mars</u> **and** <u>build habitation modules</u>.*

• to connect clauses: *<u>People will visit Mars</u>, **and** <u>they will build habitation modules</u>.*

But introduces a contrasting idea ...

• to connect words: *It's <u>hot</u> **but** <u>habitable</u>.*

• to connect phrases: *People will live <u>on Mars</u> **but** <u>not on Venus</u>.*

• to connect clauses: *<u>People will live on Mars</u>, **but** <u>they won't live on Venus</u>.*

So introduces results ...

• to connect clauses: *<u>It's very cold on Mars</u>, **so** <u>we will need to warm it up</u>.*

Remember:

• to use a comma when you connect clauses.

• when you use *and* and *but*, repeated subjects and auxiliary verbs in the second clause can be removed:

<u>People</u> <u>will</u> live on Mars. <u>People</u> <u>will</u> work on Mars.

subject   auxiliary verb   subject   auxiliary verb

*People will live **and** work on Mars.*

B Complete the sentences with *and*, *but*, or *so*.

1. Missions to Mars are expensive, _____ we probably won't send people there for many years.

2. Scientists have sent robots to the moon _____ to Mars.

3. Smart technology can help us do things more quickly _____ efficiently.

4. Scientists have an idea for warming up Mars, _____ it will take a long time before the planet is suitable for humans to live on.

5. There is no liquid water on Mars, _____ plants cannot grow there.

6. NASA wanted to send people to Mars 30 years ago, _____ the government didn't have enough money.

7. People have already been to the moon, _____ they haven't been to Mars.

8. Travel to Mars is dangerous, _____ we will send robots instead.

C Combine the sentences using *and*, *but*, or *so*. Leave out the pronoun and auxiliary verb where possible.

Example: Robots can vacuum houses. They can build cars.

<u>Robots can vacuum houses and build cars.</u>

1. PR2—a robot—can take care of elderly people. It can deliver mail.

_____

2. PR2 cooks. It doesn't communicate.

_____

3. Wakamaru knows 10,000 Japanese words. It is able to communicate with people.

_____

4. There is not enough oxygen on Mars. Humans cannot breathe there.

_____

D Work with a partner. Think of an item that will be different in the future. Think about what it will look like and how it will work. Note your ideas in the chart. Then write a sentence about the item using *and*, *but*, or *so*.

Object	What It Will Look Like / How It Will Work

_____

_____

WRITING SKILL Using Pronouns to Avoid Repetition

As you learned, pronouns usually refer to nouns that appear earlier in a text. You can use pronouns to avoid repetition.

Example: *Robots will do many things around the house. For example, robots will clean the house and prepare food.*

*Robots will do many things around the house. For example, **they** will clean the house and prepare food.*

Try not to use a pronoun that can refer to more than one thing in a sentence, as this can be confusing. For example, in the sentence "Robots will work with people, and they will become more efficient," the word "they" could refer to "robots" or "people."

E Draw a line through the repeated nouns in the sentences and replace them with suitable pronouns.

USING PRONOUNS

1. RFID chips will keep track of the food in your cabinets, and RFID chips will tell you when it's time to go to the store.

2. People on survey missions to Mars will build domes and live in the domes.

3. People will terraform Mars and make Mars more like Earth.

4. Even after a thousand years, people won't be able to breathe on Mars, so people will have to use breathing equipment.

5. Mars doesn't have any oxygen, but plants will slowly add oxygen to the atmosphere over many years.

F Read the sentences below. What does each underlined pronoun refer to? Use a word or phrase from the box. The words can be used more than once.

IDENTIFYING
PRONOUN
REFERENCE

| people | the robots | the domes | the color |

1. Sociable robots will communicate with people. <u>They</u> will speak to <u>them</u> and make eye contact with them.

they = _____   them = _____

2. People will build domes on Mars. They will live and grow plants in <u>them</u>.

them = _____

3. People will use OLED screens to change the color of their walls. If they don't like <u>it</u>, they will just push a button and change it.

it = _____

4. In the future, people will wear devices that communicate with their surroundings. The devices will provide useful information as <u>they</u> walk around the city.

they = _____

WRITING TASK

GOAL You are going to write a paragraph on the following topic:
What will a typical day be like in 2050?

BRAINSTORMING **A** Imagine a typical day in 2050. What will it be like? Brainstorm some ideas about your typical day in the future. Use these categories or your own ideas.

Study: _____

Work: _____

Travel: _____

Entertainment: _____

Other things: _____

PLANNING **B** Follow these steps to make notes for your paragraph. Don't worry about grammar or spelling. Don't write complete sentences.

Step 1 Choose three categories you want to write about (e.g., your home, work, and travel). Note them as your supporting ideas in the outline.

Step 2 Write a topic sentence for your paragraph.

Step 3 Use your brainstorming notes above to add at least one detail for each category.

OUTLINE

Topic sentence: *On a typical day in 2050,* _____

_____

Supporting Idea 1: _____

_____

Details: _____

_____

Supporting Idea 2: _____

_____

Details: _____

_____

Supporting Idea 3: _____

_____

Details: _____

_____

FIRST DRAFT **C** Use the information in your outline to write a first draft of your paragraph.

REVISING PRACTICE

The drafts below are similar to the one you are going to write, but they are on a different topic:

What will the typical home be like in 2050?

What did the writer do in Draft 2 to improve the paragraph? Match the changes (a–d) to the highlighted parts.

a. added an example to expand on a supporting idea
b. used a pronoun to avoid repetition
c. added a phrase to introduce an example
d. connected sentences with *and*, *but*, or *so*

Draft 1

A typical home in 2050 will be very different from a home of today. First of all, smart appliances will make our lives easier. Refrigerators will know how much food we have, so refrigerators will tell us when we need to go shopping. In addition, computers will control systems in the house. Finally, most homes will have robots that will help around the house. They will do important jobs, such as cleaning and cooking. They will also take care of people.

Draft 2

A typical home in 2050 will be very different from a home of today. First of all, smart appliances will make our lives easier. For example, refrigerators will know how much food we have, so they will tell us when we need to go shopping. In addition, computers will control systems in the house. For instance, computers will learn what we like and don't like, and control things around the house, such as lighting and temperature. Finally, most homes will have robots that will help around the house. They will do important jobs, such as cleaning, cooking, and taking care of people.

D Now use the questions below to revise your paragraph.

REVISED DRAFT

☐ Did you include at least one detail for each supporting idea?

☐ Do all your sentences relate to the main idea?

☐ Did you use pronouns to avoid repetition?

☐ Did you include examples?

☐ Did you connect sentences with *and*, *but*, or *so* where suitable?

EDITING PRACTICE

Read the information below.

In sentences with *and*, *but*, or *so*, remember to:
- use *and* to introduce an additional idea, *but* to introduce a contrasting idea, and *so* to introduce a result.
- use a comma when you connect two clauses.
- leave out repeated subjects and auxiliary verbs when joining ideas using *and* or *but*.

Correct one mistake with *and*, *but*, or *so* in each of the sentences (1–7).

1. People will live on Mars someday, and it is too expensive to travel there now.

2. Mars is too cold for human visitors, but scientists will need to warm it up.

3. Robots will take care of children so do housework.

4. A trip to Mars sounds amazing, and I would not like to live there!

5. Smart appliances will buy food but cook dinner.

6. We might have flying cars in 2050, and there might be fewer cars on our roads.

7. In the future, you might have a language chip in your brain but you won't have to study foreign languages.

FINAL DRAFT **E** Follow these steps to write a final draft.

1. Check your revised draft for mistakes with *and*, *but*, or *so*.

2. Now use the checklist on page 88 to write a final draft. Make any other necessary changes.

UNIT REVIEW

Answer the following questions.

1. Which prediction for the future in this unit do you think is the most interesting? Why?

_____

_____

_____

2. What are some phrases that introduce an example?

_____

_____

_____

3. Do you remember the meanings of these words? Check (✓) the ones you know. Look back at the unit and review the ones you don't know.

Reading 1:

☐ adapt AWL   ☐ intelligent AWL   ☐ link AWL

☐ network AWL   ☐ predict AWL   ☐ preference

☐ sociable   ☐ store   ☐ suggest

☐ technology AWL

Reading 2:

☐ average   ☐ environment AWL   ☐ lack

☐ level   ☐ liquid   ☐ plant

☐ release AWL   ☐ trap

SMART ADVICE

Sheryl Sandberg of Facebook delivers a speech at Tsinghua University, China.

ACADEMIC SKILLS

READING Taking notes
CRITICAL THINKING Applying an idea to a new context

THINK AND DISCUSS

1 What is the best piece of advice you have ever received?
2 Who would you talk to if you needed career advice? Why?

A Look at the information on these pages and answer the questions.

1. Which of the jobs mentioned here would you be interested in? Why?

2. Why do you think these job opportunities are increasing?

B Match the correct form of the words in blue to their definitions.

_____ (adv) in a detailed way; completely and carefully

_____ (n) a difficult task or problem

_____ (n) special skill or knowledge in a particular subject

THE FUTURE OF JOBS

A study by Economic Modeling Specialists Intl. has revealed some of the fastest growing job areas in the United States. People who are thinking about making a career change or starting their own business should research these areas thoroughly.

Leading the way is the online shopping industry, where jobs are expected to increase by 32 percent between 2016 and 2021. Some jobs in this industry include software engineer, website designer, and personal shopper.[1] Translation and interpretation services are next. People in this industry have foreign language expertise. They usually translate books and other documents, or speeches at business and government meetings. Also on the list are jobs related to environmental, conservationist, and wildlife organizations. People who work for these organizations deal with challenges like reducing pollution and protecting endangered animals.

[1] A **personal shopper** is someone who helps people shop by giving advice and making suggestions.

The fastest growing jobs
Expected job growth between 2016 and 2021 in the U.S.

Online shopping	79,919 new jobs expected	**32% increase**
Translation and interpretation services	10,547	**28%**
Physical, occupational, and speech therapy	92,217	**25%**
Environmental, conservationist, and wildlife organizations	11,833	**19%**
Computer system design services	183,682	**19%**
Nail salon services	26,987	**19%**
Pet care services	17,907	**18%**
Sports and recreation instruction	26,238	**15%**

An interpreter at the World Economic Forum, 2014

Reading 1

PREPARING TO READ

A The words in blue below are used in the reading passage on pages 71–72. Complete each sentence with the correct word. Use a dictionary to help you.

> empower   exchange   monitor   reality   promote   funding   initiative

1. A(n) _____ is the act of giving or taking one thing in return for something else.

2. _____ refers to the state of things as they actually are, as opposed to imagined or theoretical ideas.

3. If you _____ something, you check its development or progress over a period of time.

4. _____ is money that is provided for a special purpose, especially by an organization or a government.

5. To _____ a product means to encourage people to buy, use, or support it.

6. When you _____ people, you give them the ability to take more control of their lives and become stronger.

7. If you have _____, you tend to make decisions and take action without needing other people to tell you what to do.

B Discuss these questions with a partner.

1. What are your favorite subjects in school? What is your area of **expertise**?
2. What is the biggest **challenge** you have faced in school or at work? How did you overcome it?
3. What are some things a manager can do to **empower** employees?

C What three areas of your life would be most affected if you didn't have Internet access? Share your ideas with a partner.

1. _____   2. _____   3. _____

D Skim the first and last paragraphs of the reading passage on pages 71–72. Then look at the pictures and captions. What do you think Ken Banks did? Complete the sentence below. Then check your ideas as you read the passage.

I think Ken Banks created _____

that helps _____

_____

SOCIAL
ENTREPRENEURSHIP
AND INNOVATION

INTERNATIONAL CASE STUDIES
AND PRACTICE

KEN BANKS

TURNING IDEAS INTO REALITY

🎧 Track 5

The Internet has a huge influence on the lives of those who use it. It empowers people by enabling the global exchange of knowledge and information. However, many rural communities around the world still live in areas with little to no Internet access. As a result, they are largely cut off. An entrepreneur[1] named Ken Banks found a solution to this problem by using his expertise in mobile technology.

A

A SIMPLE SOLUTION TO A BIG PROBLEM

While working in South Africa in 2003 and 2004, Banks saw that there were many organizations that were trying to help local communities. Since many villages didn't have Internet access, communication was a big challenge. Banks noticed, however, that many villagers had cell phones.

B

Banks had an idea. He created some computer software called FrontlineSMS, which allows users to send information from computers without using the Internet. Users install[2] the software on a computer. Then they connect the computer to a cell phone. To send information, users select the people they want to send it to. The cell phone sends the information to groups of people as a text message. Individuals can then reply on their own cell phones, creating a two-way messaging system between phone users and the computer.

C

[1] An **entrepreneur** is a person who starts a business.
[2] When you **install** a computer program, you set it up or connect it for use on your computer.

D FrontlineSMS is free and can work almost anywhere in the world. In Malawi, a rural healthcare program uses it to contact patients. As a result, health workers no longer have to visit patients' homes to update medical records or pass along important information. The software has also been used to monitor elections in Nigeria and to help disaster relief efforts in Haiti. Today, it is used in over 190 countries.

CREATING A SUCCESSFUL PRODUCT

E FrontlineSMS is a good example of taking an idea and making it a reality. So what should you do if you have an idea for making the world a better place? Banks offers the following advice:

F Don't immediately try to get money—most donors[3] want to see that you have a good idea first. "[D]onors don't tend to respond so well to people who just reach for money without actually showing they can do something," Banks explains. So start by researching your idea or product thoroughly. Do people really need it? To find out if you have a good idea, go into the community and talk to people.

G Once you have a workable idea, promote it. Use all the social media tools that you can: Start a Facebook group, use Twitter, or create a website. Start a blog and write about what you're doing. Connect online with other people who are working in the same field as you. The more you post, the easier it will be for search engines to find you.

H If you have a good idea, and you've gotten your message out, people will notice you. Now is the time to try to get funding. Your social networks are a good place to start raising money. Waiting until you have gotten this far shows potential donors that you have initiative, Banks says. It also shows that you are committed.

I We're currently living in the best time to create a product that can reach millions of people. More and more entrepreneurs are developing and promoting products that have the potential to solve the world's greatest challenges. All you need is an idea. As Banks puts it, "Innovation ... is about someone standing in a rural village somewhere and suddenly realizing, 'If I did this ... *that* could happen.'"

[3]A **donor** is a person or group that gives something (e.g., money) to help a person or organization.

▶ "FrontlineSMS gives [people] tools to create their own projects and make a difference," Banks says.

UNDERSTANDING THE READING

A Choose the best alternative title for the reading passage.

UNDERSTANDING
THE MAIN IDEA

    a. Innovative Solutions to Improve the World
    b. Tips for Managing a Business in a Developing Country
    c. A Day in the Life of an Entrepreneur

B Answer the questions below using information from the reading passage.

UNDERSTANDING
DETAILS

    1. What gave Ken Banks the idea for FrontlineSMS?

    _____

    2. Why is FrontlineSMS a good solution for developing countries?

    _____

    3. What is one example of how FrontlineSMS has been used?

    _____

    4. According to Banks, what should you do if you have an idea for making the world a better place? Summarize his three steps.

        a. _____

        b. _____

        c. _____

C How does FrontlineSMS work? Number the steps from 1 to 5 to show the correct sequence.

IDENTIFYING
SEQUENCE

    _____ Cell phone users can reply to the text message.

    _____ The cell phone sends information as a text message from the computer.

    _____ Then they connect a cell phone to the computer.

    _____ Users select the people they want to send information to.

    _____ Users install the FrontlineSMS software on a computer.

> **CRITICAL THINKING**   **Applying an idea** to another real-world situation can help you evaluate the pros and cons of that idea. Ask yourself: In what situation(s) would that idea be useful? Who would benefit most from it?

D How might FrontlineSMS be used to solve the following problems? Which situation would it be more useful for? Discuss your ideas in small groups.

CRITICAL THINKING:
APPLYING AN IDEA
TO A NEW CONTEXT

    1. to protect an endangered animal
    2. to help children who don't have access to education

E The writer states, "We're currently living in the best time to create a product that can reach millions of people." Why do you think this is? Discuss with a partner.

CRITICAL THINKING:
INFERRING

DEVELOPING READING SKILLS

> **READING SKILL** Taking Notes
>
> Taking notes on a reading passage is a useful skill. One method of taking notes is to use different types of graphic organizers to help organize the ideas in a reading.
>
> Another note-taking method is to identify the main idea and the supporting details of each paragraph, or section, as you read. If you read a long or difficult passage, you may forget some of the important ideas soon after you have finished reading. Summarizing the main ideas and details in a chart will help you review the content more easily later.
>
> When completing a summary chart, remember to note only the key points. Don't write complete sentences. Try to use your own words as much as possible.

TAKING NOTES **A** Complete the following chart with notes on "Turning Ideas into Reality" (pages 71–72).

Paragraph	Main Idea	Details
B	*how Banks got the idea for FrontlineSMS*	*- lived in S. Africa in 2003–04* *- trouble communicating w/out Internet, but had cell phones*
C		
D		
F		
G		
H		

APPLYING **B** Use the notes you took in exercise A to write a summary of "Turning Ideas into Reality."

Video

Martín Andrade (kneeling) with local children at a project site in Chile

THE COMMUNITY BUILDER

BEFORE VIEWING

A Read the information about Martín Andrade and his foundation. Then answer the questions.

LEARNING ABOUT THE TOPIC

The World Health Organization (WHO) recommends 9 square meters of green space per person. However, in certain urban areas of Chile, the reality falls short of this recommendation. While working as an architect in Santiago, Martín Andrade became aware that most of the public spaces in the city's poor areas were dirty and ugly. Many families didn't have access to beautiful green parks where they could spend time with their loved ones or enjoy nature. Andrade believed that if nothing was done to improve these public spaces, future generations born into this environment would be more vulnerable[1] to drug and alcohol abuse. He and a few other architects therefore started a foundation with the aim of improving the lives of low-income Chilean families. Because of his work, Andrade was named Chile's "Social Entrepreneur of the Year" in 2012.

[1]If you are **vulnerable** to something, you can be easily harmed or affected by it.

1. What problem did Andrade notice in Chile?

   _____

2. What is the goal of his foundation?

   _____

3. How do you think the foundation attempts to achieve this goal?

   _____

B Below are some quotes from the video. Match the correct form of each **bold** word or phrase to its definition.

> "… the scenery in many places is **breathtaking**."
>
> "Mi Parque … was **founded** by Martín Andrade and a few other architects."
>
> "Don't let the big problems facing society **get you down**."

1. _____ (v) to set up or establish (an institution or organization)

2. _____ (v) to make you feel sad or lose hope

3. _____ (adj) extremely beautiful or amazing

WHILE VIEWING

A ▶ Watch the video. Check (✓) the topics that are discussed.

☐ 1. how Andrade's career as an architect began

☐ 2. the lack of green space in some Chilean communities

☐ 3. how the foundation gathered construction materials for its first park

☐ 4. the foundation's plans to expand to other countries

B ▶ Watch the video again and answer the questions below.

1. What was one of the biggest challenges Andrade faced in getting his foundation started?

   _____

2. Which achievement is Andrade most proud of?

   _____

3. What two pieces of advice does Andrade give to people who want to start their own foundation?

   a. _____

   b. _____

AFTER VIEWING

A How might increasing people's access to green spaces improve their quality of life? Discuss your ideas with a partner.

B In the video, Andrade says:

"If you're focused on the resources that you currently have, you'll find that there are simple things that you can do now to make the world a better place."

What are some "simple things" that can make a difference? Find three examples from this book or use your own ideas. Discuss with a partner.

Reading 2

PREPARING TO READ

A The words in **blue** below are used in the reading passage on pages 78–79. Complete each sentence with the correct form of the word. Use a dictionary to help you.

BUILDING
VOCABULARY

passion	sensible	defining	consumer
quality	worth	reputation	demanding

1. A _____ person shows good judgment and makes careful decisions.

2. Given the rise in college fees, some students aren't sure if getting a college education is _____ the cost.

3. When choosing a college, students will usually think about whether the school has a good academic _____ .

4. Many _____ who own Apple products are very loyal. They are more likely to buy Apple products than similar items from other companies.

5. One way to figure out what type of career you will enjoy is to think about what activities you love doing and have a _____ for.

6. People who are _____ are not easily satisfied or pleased.

7. Graduating from college is a _____ moment for many people. It usually marks the time when people first enter the workforce.

8. Attention to detail is an important factor in making sure that products are of the highest _____ .

B Discuss these questions with a partner.

USING
VOCABULARY

1. Besides graduating from college, what are some other **defining** moments in our lives?
2. What are some brands that are known for having excellent product **quality**?
3. Who is the most **sensible** person you know? Describe that person.

C The reading passage on pages 78–79 is about business lessons that Guy Kawasaki has learned throughout his career. Scan the reading passage for the lessons he has learned, and note them below. Then check your answers as you read the passage.

PREDICTING

_____

_____

_____

LESSONS IN BUSINESS

Tech entrepreneur Guy Kawasaki speaks at a festival in Austin, Texas.

🎧 Track 6

A Guy Kawasaki is perhaps best known for his efforts in promoting Apple's early products like the Macintosh computer. He has since gone on to build a career as a successful entrepreneur, author, and speaker. Along the way, he has learned many important lessons from the people he's worked with.

B After receiving his M.B.A. from UCLA in 1979, Kawasaki entered the jewelry business. The president of the company he worked for was a man named Martin Gruber. One of the biggest lessons Kawasaki learned from Gruber was how to sell a product. "It's not about selling a commodity[1] or the features of a product but to sell the benefits," Kawasaki says. This lesson proved to be valuable in his next job at Apple.

C Working at Apple was the turning point in Kawasaki's life. At the time, the company was just starting to take off. Kawasaki gave himself the job title "chief evangelist." As an evangelist, he promoted Apple's products and shared his **passion** for them with other people.

D Kawasaki learned how to handle office politics from Al Eisenstat, general counsel[2] at Apple. "[Eisenstat] showed me how corporate politics works—to not burn your bridges and to be nice to everyone," he explains. This **sensible** piece of advice helped Kawasaki during a power struggle between the company's leaders in the mid-80s.

[1]A **commodity** is a product (as opposed to a service) that is sold for money.
[2]A **general counsel** is a company's chief lawyer.

Another leader who influenced Kawasaki was Steve Jobs, co-founder of Apple. Kawasaki worked for Jobs—a famously tough boss—not once, but twice. He has described working for Jobs as one of the defining experiences of his life. Here are four things Kawasaki learned from the Apple boss:

People cannot describe their needs. Customers often don't know what they want until they see it. For example, the first Apple computer was very different from the personal computers available at the time. Customers didn't know they needed something different until Apple created it. A successful entrepreneur identifies problems that need solving before anyone else does.

Design counts. *Simple. Elegant. Fun.* All these words describe Apple's design philosophy. Apple products are well-known for their beautiful design, and enjoy great sales as a result. If your product looks good, consumers will be more likely to buy it, even if the price is high. An attractive design tells consumers that a product is of good quality and is worth the price.

You get the best results when you give people big goals. Don't simplify things for employees; give them big challenges instead. Jobs was well-known for his attention to detail. In fact, he had a reputation for being a very demanding boss. But, as Kawasaki explains, "I, and Apple employees before me and after me, did their best work because we had to do our best work to meet the big challenges."

Most experts are clueless. Experts—including consultants, analysts, and journalists—are often disconnected from customers. So don't trust the experts—their opinions aren't always accurate. As Kawasaki puts it, "Steve Jobs did not listen to experts ... [E]xperts listened to him." Kawasaki advises entrepreneurs to do their own research and to reach out to consumers directly. The best way to do this, he says, is by using social media.

▼ **Apple co-founder Steve Jobs, 1988**

SELLING A PRODUCT

Here are four tips from Guy Kawasaki on using social media to sell a product:

1. Post frequently.

2. Post things that improve people's lives.

3. Include a video or a picture with every post.

4. Repeat your posts, because people live in different time zones and work on different schedules.

UNDERSTANDING THE READING

UNDERSTANDING
THE MAIN IDEA

A What is the main purpose of the reading passage?

a.   to explain why Steve Jobs was a great boss
b.   to describe what it is like to work for Apple
c.   to share important business lessons from Guy Kawasaki

IDENTIFYING
OPINIONS

B Would Guy Kawasaki agree with the following statements? Circle **Y** (Yes), **N** (No), or **NG** (Not Given) if there isn't enough information in the reading passage.

1.   When selling a product, it's more important to describe its features than its benefits.   Y   N   NG

2.   Entrepreneurs should design products based on what consumers say they want.   Y   N   NG

3.   Consumers are more likely to value design over price.   Y   N   NG

4.   Entrepreneurs should keep environmental issues in mind when designing a product.   Y   N   NG

5.   It's important to give employees challenging tasks.   Y   N   NG

6.   It's important to rely on experts if you're starting a business.   Y   N   NG

7.   When using social media to promote something, you should post the same information more than once.   Y   N   NG

CRITICAL THINKING:
INFERRING MEANING

C Find and underline the following **bold** words and phrases in the reading passage. Use context to identify their meanings. Then match each word or phrase to its definition.

turning point (paragraph C)   **power struggle** (paragraph D)
take off (paragraph C)   **philosophy** (paragraph G)
burn your bridges (paragraph D)   **clueless** (paragraph I)

1.   _____ (n) a fight for control between two or more people

2.   _____ (n) a time when an important change happens

3.   _____ (n) a set of ideas about how to do something

4.   _____ (adj) having no knowledge about a particular subject

5.   _____ (v) to suddenly start being successful

6.   _____ (v) to do something that makes it impossible to return to an earlier situation or relationship

CRITICAL THINKING:
SYNTHESIZING

D Compare the advice given by Ken Banks, Martín Andrade, and Guy Kawasaki. What similarities or differences do you see? Discuss with a partner.

UNIT REVIEW

Answer the following questions.

1. Which piece of advice in this unit do you find most helpful? Why?

   _____

   _____

2. How could you use this unit's reading skill outside of class?

   _____

   _____

3. Do you remember the meanings of these words? Check (✓) the ones you know. Look back at the unit and review the ones you don't know.

   Reading 1:

   ☐ challenge AWL ☐ empower   ☐ exchange
   ☐ expertise AWL ☐ funding AWL ☐ initiative AWL
   ☐ monitor AWL   ☐ promote AWL ☐ reality
   ☐ thoroughly

   Reading 2:

   ☐ consumer AWL ☐ defining AWL ☐ demanding
   ☐ passion   ☐ quality   ☐ reputation
   ☐ sensible   ☐ worth

VOCABULARY EXTENSION UNIT 1

WORD LINK *dis-*

The prefix *dis-* can be added to some verbs, nouns, and adjectives to create an opposite or negative meaning. For example, *disorganized* means "not organized" or "messy."

A Circle the best word to complete each sentence.

1. Some people **disbelieve / dislike** rock music. They think it's too loud.

2. My friends have strong **disagreements / disadvantages** about which band is the best.

3. The sound of classical music and pop music is **dissimilar / disinterested** in many ways.

4. Some parents think it's a **disagreement / disadvantage** for children not to learn a musical instrument.

5. Although Stevie Wonder couldn't see, he didn't let his **disability / distrust** stop him from learning several musical instruments and becoming a famous artist.

WORD FORMS Changing Adjectives into Nouns

Some adjectives can be changed into nouns by adding *-ity*. For adjectives ending in *-ble*, replace *-le* with *-ility*.

ADJECTIVE	NOUN
similar	*similarity*
responsible	*responsibility*

B Complete each sentence with the correct noun form of the adjectives below.

adaptable   electric   popular   possible   responsible

1. The _____ of rap music continues to increase among young people.

2. Some musicians feel they have a(n) _____ to use their influence and create positive change.

3. Some modern musical instruments, like keyboards, require _____ to produce sound.

4. People's music preferences can change quickly, so _____ is an important quality in order for musicians to succeed.

5. In the future, there is a(n) _____ that people will only listen to music through online music streaming services.

VOCABULARY EXTENSION UNIT 3

Some adjectives end in the suffix *-able* which means "able to." For example, *sociable* means "able to be social."

A Circle the correct form of the word to complete each sentence.

1. Social robots are **suit** / **suitable** to use even with very young children.

2. Experts **predict** / **predictable** that smart technology will be a big part of our lives in the future.

3. These days, some phones allow people to use their voice to **control** / **controllable** functions like doing a search online or writing an email.

4. I would like a robot that is **adapt** / **adaptable** to different tasks, such as cooking, cleaning, and taking care of a pet.

5. Not everyone may feel **comfort** / **comfortable** with using new forms of technology.

WORD FORMS Changing Verbs into Nouns

	VERB	NOUN
Adding *-ment* to some verbs can change them into nouns. A noun with the suffix *-ment* means "the action or result" of doing the verb.	*move*	*movement*
	equip	*equipment*

B Complete each sentence with the correct noun form of the words below.

> assign   equip   govern   measure   state

1. People need special _____ to help them breathe on Mars.

2. In 2010, the U.S. _____ gave NASA permission to develop manned missions to Mars.

3. In a recent _____ , NASA said they plan to put humans on Mars by 2040.

4. Today, scientists are taking _____ on Mars's surface to better understand the planet's environment.

5. NASA announces their crew _____ on its website by posting a list of people who are going to be working at the International Space Station.

VOCABULARY EXTENSION   UNIT 4

Below are some common expressions with the word *challenge*.

If a task **presents a challenge**, it appears to be difficult.

If you **meet a challenge**, you overcome or complete a difficult problem.

If a task is a **big challenge**, it is very difficult to do.

If you are looking for a **fresh challenge**, you are looking for something new and difficult to do.

A Complete each sentence using the correct form of a word from the box below.

> big   fresh   meet   present

1. Climbing Mount Everest _____ a challenge for many climbers.

2. Edmund Hillary and Tenzing Norgay _____ that challenge when they became the first people to climb Everest in 1953.

3. Climbing a 40-foot vertical rock at the top of Everest was a _____ challenge for Hillary and Norgay.

4. After climbing Everest, Hillary wanted a _____ challenge, so he started an organization to build schools and hospitals for the Sherpa people of Nepal.

Below are some common expressions with the word *quality*.

Quality of life is how good or bad a person's life is.

Air quality is the degree to which the air in a particular place is pollution-free.

Star quality is a special ability that makes someone seem better than other people.

If you spend **quality time** with someone, you give them all of your attention.

B Write a sentence in response to each prompt. Use the **bold** expressions in your answers.

1. One way to improve your **quality of life**

_____

2. One way to improve **air quality** in your city

_____

3. Someone you think has **star quality**

_____

4. Someone you like to spend **quality time** with

_____

GRAMMAR REFERENCE

UNIT 1
Language for Writing: Using Time Expressions

Use prepositions of time to show what happened in a person's life.

Notes	Examples
Use *in* for months, years, and specific periods of time.	Yo-Yo Ma was born in Paris **in** 1955.
Use *on* for specific dates.	**On** July 5, 1986, Ma performed a concert in New York City.
Use *before* for an earlier time.	Ma lived in Paris **before** 1962.
Use *after* for a later time.	**After** 1962, Ma moved to New York.
Use *during* to indicate a period of time an event or events happened for.	**During** the concert, Ma played the cello.

Time clauses help show the order of events in someone's life. A time clause includes time words such as *after*, *before*, and *when*.

Notes	Examples
Use a comma after the time clause.	TIME CLAUSE **After** <u>Ma moved to New York</u>, he attended the Julliard School of Music.
A time clause can come at the end of a sentence. No comma is needed.	Ma attended the Julliard School of Music **after** <u>he moved to New York</u>.
Use *after* to show the first event. Use *before* to show the next event.	**After** Ma moved to New York, he attended the Julliard School of Music. **Before** Ma attended the Julliard School of Music, he moved to New York. (First he moved to New York, then he attended the Julliard School of Music.)
Use *when* to show the time an event first started.	He started playing the cello **when he was 4 years old**. **When he was 4 years old**, he learned to play the cello.

UNIT 3
Language for Writing: Coordinating Conjunctions

And, but, and *so* are coordinating conjunctions. They can connect single words, phrases, or clauses.

Notes	Example
Use *and* to connect or add information.	Students are studying Mars **and** Venus.
	People will visit Mars **and** build habitation modules.
	People will visit Mars, **and** they will build habitation modules.
Use *but* to show contrast.	Mars is cold **but** habitable.
	People have traveled to the moon **but** not to Mars.
	People have traveled to the moon, **but** they haven't traveled to Mars.
Use *so* to show result.	It is very cold on Mars, **so** we will need to warm it up.
Remove repeated subjects in the second clause.	Mars is very cold **and** (~~Mars~~) has no oxygen.
Remove repeated verbs and auxiliary verbs in the second clause.	People will live **and** (~~will~~) work on Mars.

UNIT 4
Language for Writing: Using the Zero Conditional to Give Advice

A zero conditional sentence includes an *if* clause and a result (or main) clause. In zero conditional sentences, we use the simple present tense in both clauses.

We usually use zero conditional sentences to describe general truths and facts.

If Clause (Condition)	Main Clause (Result)
If you heat ice,	it melts.
If a company goes out of business,	employees lose their jobs.
If someone gets promoted,	they receive a higher salary.

The zero conditional is often used with modal verbs to give advice. Include the modal verb in the result clause. The modal expresses ability, necessity, or permission. In the zero conditional sentence structure, you can use *should* or *can*, and their negative forms.

If Clause (Condition)	Main Clause (Result)
If you want to go to university,	you **should study** hard.
If you drink,	you **shouldn't drive**.
If you need advice about what to do,	you **can call** Bill.
If you have celiac disease,	you **can't eat** wheat.

We can also use the zero conditional with imperative verbs to give advice. Include the imperative verb in the result clause. These sentences are similar to saying: If the condition occurs, you must do this (in the result clause).

If Clause (Condition)	Main Clause (Result)
If you don't want to get lost,	**follow** the directions carefully.
If you want to be healthier,	**eat** less junk food and **exercise** more.
If you drink,	**don't drive**.

When the *if* clause appears at the end of a sentence, there is no comma between the clauses.

Main Clause (Result)	*If* Clause (Condition)
Employees lose their jobs	if a company goes out of business.
You should study hard	if you want to go to university.
Follow the directions carefully	if you don't want to get lost.

EDITING CHECKLIST

Use the checklist to find errors in your writing task for each unit.

	WRITING TASK	
	1	2
1. Is the first word of every sentence capitalized?		
2. Does every sentence end with the correct punctuation?		
3. Do your subjects and verbs agree?		
4. Are commas used in the right places?		
5. Do all possessive nouns have an apostrophe?		
6. Are all proper nouns capitalized?		
7. Is the spelling of places, people, and other proper nouns correct?		
8. Did you check for frequently confused words?		

Brief Writer's Handbook

Understanding the Writing Process: The Seven Steps

The Assignment

Imagine that you have been given the following assignment: *Write a definition paragraph about an everyday item.*

What should you do first? What should you do second, third, and so on? There are many ways to write, but most good writers follow certain general steps in the writing process.

Look at this list of steps. Which ones do you usually do? Which ones have you never done?

> STEP 1: Choose a topic.
>
> STEP 2: Brainstorm.
>
> STEP 3: Outline.
>
> STEP 4: Write the first draft.
>
> STEP 5: Get feedback from a peer.
>
> STEP 6: Revise the first draft.
>
> STEP 7: Proofread the final draft.

Now you will see how one student went through all the steps to do the assignment. First, read the final paragraph that Susan gave her teacher. Read the teacher's comments as well.

Example Paragraph 1

Gumbo

The dictionary definition of *gumbo* does not make gumbo sound as delicious as it really is. The dictionary defines gumbo as a "thick soup made in south Louisiana." However, anyone who has tasted this delicious dish knows that this definition is too bland to describe gumbo. It is true that gumbo is a thick soup, but it is much more than that. Gumbo, one of the most popular of all Cajun dishes, is made with different kinds of seafood or meat mixed with vegetables, such as green peppers and onions. For example, seafood gumbo contains shrimp and crab. Other kinds of gumbo include chicken, sausage, or turkey. Regardless of the ingredients in gumbo, this regional delicacy is very delicious.

Teacher comments:

100/A⁺   Excellent paragraph!
I enjoyed reading about gumbo. Your paragraph is very well written. All the sentences relate to one single topic. I really like the fact that you used so many connectors—however, such as.

Now look at the steps that Susan went through to compose the paragraph that you just read.

Steps in the Writing Process

Step 1: Choose a Topic

Susan chose gumbo as her topic. This is what she wrote about her choice.

When I first saw the assignment, I did not know what to write about. I did not think I was going to be able to find a good topic.

First, I tried to think of something that I could define. It could not be something that was really simple like television or a car. Everyone already knows what they are. I thought that I should choose something that most people might not know.

I tried to think of general areas like sports, machines, and inventions. However, I chose food as my general area. Everyone likes food.

Then I had to find one kind of food that not everyone knows. For me, that was not too difficult. My family is from Louisiana, and the food in Louisiana is special. It is not the usual food that most Americans eat. One of the dishes we eat a lot in Louisiana is gumbo, which is a kind of thick soup. I thought gumbo would be a good topic for a definition paragraph because not many people know it, and it is sort of easy for me to write a definition for this food.

Another reason that gumbo is a good choice for a definition paragraph is that I know a lot about this kind of food. I know how to make it, I know what the ingredients are, and I know what it tastes like. It is much easier to write about something that I know than about something that I do not know about.

After I was sure that gumbo was going to be my topic, I went on to the next step, which is brainstorming.

Susan's notes about choosing her topic

Step 2: Brainstorm

The next step for Susan was to brainstorm ideas about her topic.

In this step, you write down every idea that pops into your head about your topic. Some of these ideas will be good, and some will be bad—write them all down. The main purpose of brainstorming is to write down as many ideas as you can think of. If one idea looks especially good, you might circle that idea or put a check mark next to it. If you write down an idea and you know right away that you are not going to use it, you can cross it out.

Look at Susan's brainstorming diagram on the topic of gumbo.

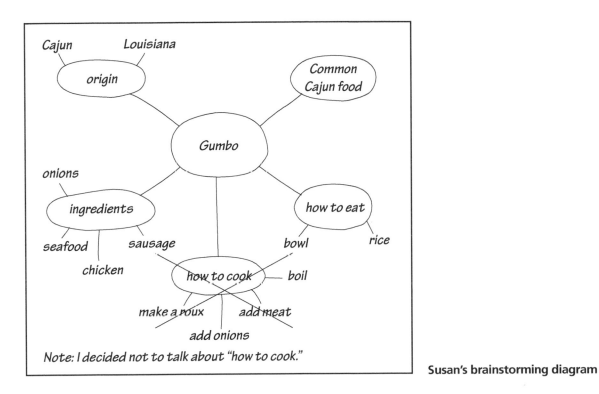

Note: I decided not to talk about "how to cook."

Susan's brainstorming diagram

Step 3: Outline

At this point, some writers want to start writing, but that is not the best plan. After you brainstorm your ideas, the next step is to make an outline. An outline helps you organize how you will present your information. It helps you see which areas of the paragraph are strong and which are weak.

After brainstorming, Susan studied her list of ideas. She then made a simple outline of what her paragraph might look like. Some writers prepare very detailed outlines, but many writers just make a list of the main points and some of the details for each main point.

Read the outline that Susan wrote.

What is gumbo?
1. A simple definition of gumbo.
2. A longer definition of gumbo.
3. A list of the different ingredients of gumbo.
  A. seafood or meat
  B. with vegetables (onions)
  C. seafood gumbo
4. How gumbo is served.

Susan's outline

As you can see, this outline is very basic. There are also some problems. For example, Susan repeats some items in different parts of the outline. In addition, she does not have a concluding sentence. These errors will probably be corrected at the first draft step, the peer editing step, or the final draft step.

Step 4: Write the First Draft

Next, Susan wrote a first draft. In this step, you use the information from your outline and from your brainstorming session to write a first draft. This first draft may contain many errors, such as misspellings, incomplete ideas, and incorrect punctuation. At this point, do not worry about correcting the errors. The main goal is to put your ideas into sentences.

You may feel that you do not know what you think about the topic yet. In this case, it may be difficult for you to write, but it is important to start the process of writing. Sometimes writing helps you think, and as soon as you form a new thought, you can write it down.

Read Susan's first draft, including her notes to herself.

Introduction is weak ??? Use dictionary!

(Rough draft)
Susan Mims

Do you know what gumbo is. It's a seafood soup. However, gumbo is really more than a kind of soup, it's special. ???

Gumbo is one of the most popular of all Cajun dish. es

Combine { *It's made with various kind of seafood or meet. meat*
This is mixed with vegetables such as onions. green peppers

Combine { *Seafood Gumbo is made with shrimp and crab.*
Also chicken, sausage, and turkey, etc. Regardless ok ??? of what is in Gumbo, it's usually served in bowl a over the rice.
— Is this correct? Ask teacher!

Susan's first draft

What do you notice about this first draft? Here are a few things that a good writer should pay attention to:

- First of all, remember that this paper is not the final draft. Even native speakers who are good writers usually write more than one draft. You will have a chance to revise the paper and make it better.

- Look at the circles, question marks, and writing in the margin. These are notes that Susan made to herself about what to change, add, or reconsider.

- Remember that the paper will go through the peer-editing process later. Another reader will help you make your meaning clear and will look for errors.

In addition to the language errors that writers often make in the first draft, the handwriting is usually not neat. Sometimes it is so messy that only the writer can read it!

Step 5: Get Feedback from a Peer

Peer editing a draft is a critical step toward the final goal of excellent writing. Sometimes it is difficult for writers to see the weaknesses in their own writing, so receiving advice from another writer can be very helpful.

Ask a colleague, friend, or classmate to read your writing and to offer suggestions about how to improve it. Some people do not like criticism, but constructive criticism is always helpful for writers. Remember that even professional writers have editors, so do not be embarrassed to receive help.

Susan exchanged papers with another student, Jim, in her class. On the next page is the peer editing sheet that Jim completed about Susan's paragraph. Read the questions and answers.

Peer Editing Sheet

Writer: __Susan__ Date: __2-14__

Peer Editor: __Jim__

1. What is the general topic of the paper? __gumbo__

2. What is the writer's purpose? (in 15 words or less)

   __to define gumbo__

3. Is the paragraph indented? ☑ yes ☐ no

4. How many sentences are there? __6__

5. Is the first word of every sentence capitalized? ☑ yes ☐ no
   If you answered *no,* circle the problem(s) on the paper.

6. Does every sentence end with correct punctuation? ☐ yes ☑ no
   If you answered *no,* circle the problem(s) on the paper.

7. Are there any other capitalization or punctuation errors? ☑ yes ☐ no
   If you answered *yes,* circle the problem(s) on the paper.

8. Write the topic sentence here.

   __You have two sentences: Do you know what gumbo is. It is a seafood soup.__

9. Do you think the topic sentence is good for this paragraph? Comments?

   __No, you need one sentence that introduces your topic and purpose better.__

10. Does the paragraph talk about just one topic? ☑ yes ☐ no

    If you answered *no,* what is the extra topic? _____

    In what sentence is this extra topic introduced? _____

11. Does every sentence have a verb? ❑ yes ☑ no

If you answered *no,* circle the error(s)on the paper.

12. Write any mistakes that you found. Add appropriate corrections.

Error 1: _it's-don't use contractions in formal writing_

Correction: _it is_

Error 2: _etc.-don't use this_

Correction: _You should list all the kinds._

Error 3: _____

Correction: _____

13. Did you have any trouble understanding this paragraph? ❑ yes ☑ no

If you answered *yes,* tell where and/or why.

_____

14. What questions do you have about the content? What other information should be in this paragraph?

How do you make gumbo? Is it easy to cook? Why do you think people started making gumbo?

15. What is your opinion of the writing of this paragraph?

It is good, but the concluding sentence gives new information. It does not conclude! Also,

do not repeat the word "gumbo" so much. Do not use "is" so much! Use other verbs.

16. What is your opinion of the content of this paragraph?

I like the topic. I think I ate gumbo at a restaurant once.

Step 6: Revise the First Draft

In this step, you will see how Susan used the suggestions and information to revise her paragraph. This step consists of three parts:

1. React to the comments on the peer editing sheet.

2. Reread the paragraph and make changes.

3. Rewrite the paragraph one more time.

Here is what Susan wrote about the changes she decided to make.

> I read my paragraph again several times. Each time I read it, I found things that I wanted to change in some way. Sometimes I corrected an obvious error. Other times I added words to make my writing clear to the reader. Based on Jim's suggestion, I used "this delicious dish" and other expressions instead of repeating "gumbo" so many times.
>
> I used some of Jim's suggestions, but I did not use all of them. I thought that some of his questions were interesting, but the answers were not really part of the purpose of this paragraph, which was to define gumbo.
>
> I was happy that the peer editor was able to understand all my ideas fully. To me, this means that my writing is good enough.

Susan's notes about changes she decided to make

Step 7: Proofread the Final Draft

Most of the hard work should be over by now. In this step, the writer pretends to be a brand-new reader who has never seen the paper before. The writer reads the paper to see if the sentences and ideas flow smoothly.

Read Susan's final paper again on page 89. Notice any changes in vocabulary, grammar, spelling, or punctuation that she made at this stage.

Of course, the very last step is to turn the paper in to your teacher and hope that you get a good grade!

Editing Your Writing

While you must be comfortable writing quickly, you also need to be comfortable with improving your work. Writing an assignment is never a one-step process. For even the most gifted writers, it is often a multiple-step process. When you were completing your assignments in this book, you probably made some changes to your work to make it better. However, you may not have fixed all of the errors. The paper that you turned in to your teacher is called a **first draft,** which is sometimes referred to as a **rough draft.**

A first draft can almost always be improved. One way to improve your writing is to ask a classmate, friend, or teacher to read it and make suggestions. Your reader may discover that one of your paragraphs is missing a topic sentence, that you have made grammar mistakes, or that your essay needs different vocabulary choices. You may not always like or agree with the comments from a reader, but being open to changes will make you a better writer.

This section will help you become more familiar with how to identify and correct errors in your writing.

Step 1

Below is a student's first draft for a timed writing. The writing prompt for this assignment, was "Many schools now offer classes online. Which do you prefer and why?" As you read the first draft, look for areas that need improvement and write your comments. For example, does every sentence have a subject and a verb? Does the writer always use the correct verb tense and punctuation? Does the paragraph have a topic sentence with controlling ideas? Is the vocabulary suitable for the intended audience? What do you think of the content?

The Online Courses

Online courses are very popular at my university. I prefered traditional face-to-face classes. At my university, students have a choice between courses that are taught online in a virtual classroom and the regular kind of classroom. I know that many students prefer online classes, but I cannot adjust to that style of educate. For me, is important to have a professor who explains the material to everyone "live" and then answer any questions that we have. Sometimes students might think they understand the material until the professor questions, and then we realize that we did not understand everything. At that moment, the professor then offers other explanation to help bridge the gap. I do not see this kind of spontaneous learning and teaching can take place online. I have never taken an online course until now. Some of my friends like online courses because they can take the class at his own convenience instead of have to assist class at a set time. However, these supposed conveniences are not outweigh the educational advantages that traditional face-to-face classes offer.

Step 2

Read the teacher comments on the first draft of "The Online Courses." Are these the same things that you noticed?

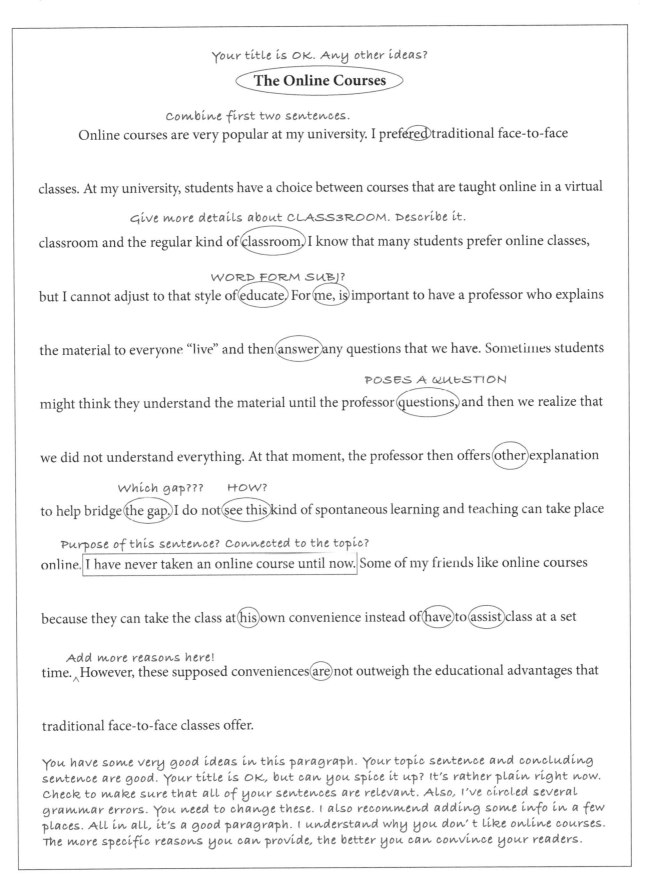

Your title is OK. Any other ideas?

The Online Courses

Combine first two sentences.

Online courses are very popular at my university. I prefered traditional face-to-face

classes. At my university, students have a choice between courses that are taught online in a virtual

Give more details about CLASS3ROOM. Describe it.

classroom and the regular kind of classroom. I know that many students prefer online classes,

WORD FORM SUBJ?

but I cannot adjust to that style of educate. For me, is important to have a professor who explains

the material to everyone "live" and then answer any questions that we have. Sometimes students

POSES A QUESTION

might think they understand the material until the professor questions, and then we realize that

we did not understand everything. At that moment, the professor then offers other explanation

Which gap???   HOW?

to help bridge the gap. I do not see this kind of spontaneous learning and teaching can take place

Purpose of this sentence? Connected to the topic?

online. I have never taken an online course until now. Some of my friends like online courses

because they can take the class at his own convenience instead of have to assist class at a set

Add more reasons here!

time. However, these supposed conveniences are not outweigh the educational advantages that

traditional face-to-face classes offer.

You have some very good ideas in this paragraph. Your topic sentence and concluding sentence are good. Your title is OK, but can you spice it up? It's rather plain right now. Check to make sure that all of your sentences are relevant. Also, I've circled several grammar errors. You need to change these. I also recommend adding some info in a few places. All in all, it's a good paragraph. I understand why you don't like online courses. The more specific reasons you can provide, the better you can convince your readers.

Step 3

Now read the writer's second draft of the paragraph. How is it the same as the first draft? How is it different? Did the writer fix all the sentence mistakes?

Online Courses

Online courses are very popular at my university but I prefer traditional face-to-face classes. At my university students have a choice between courses that are taught online in a virtual classroom and the regular kind of classroom with a room, a professor, and students in chairs. I know that many students prefer online classes, but I cannot adjust to that style of education. For me, it is important to have a professor who explains the material to everyone "live" and then answers any questions that we might have. Sometimes students might think they understand the material until the professor poses a question, and then we realize that we did not understand everything. At that moment, the professor then offers another explanation to help bridge the gap between our knowledge and the truth. I do not see how this kind of spontaneous leaerning and teaching can take place online. Some of my friends like online courses because they can take the class at their own convenience instead of having to attend class at a set time. They also like to save transportation money and time. However, these supposed conveniences do not outweigh the many educational advantages that traditional face-to-face classes offer.

Capitalization Activities
Basic Capitalization Rules

1. Always capitalize the first word of a sentence.

   > Today is not Sunday.

   > It is not Saturday either.

   > Do you know today's date?

2. Always capitalize the word *I* no matter where it is in a sentence.

   > John brought the dessert, and I brought some drinks.

   > I want some tea.

   > The winners of the contest were Ned and I.

3. Capitalize proper nouns—the names of specific people, places, or things. Capitalize a person's title, including Mr., Mrs., Ms., and Dr. Compare these example pairs.

   Proper nouns: When our teacher **Mr. H**ill visited his home state of **A**rizona, he took a short trip to see the **G**rand **C**anyon.

   Common nouns: When our teacher visited his home state, he saw many mountains and canyons.

   Proper nouns: The **S**tatue of **L**iberty is located on **L**iberty **I**sland in **N**ew **Y**ork.

   Common nouns: There is a famous statue on that island, isn't there?

4. Capitalize names of countries and other geographic areas. Capitalize the names of people from those areas. Capitalize the names of languages.

   > People from **B**razil are called **B**razilians. They speak **P**ortuguese.

   > People from **G**ermany are called **G**ermans. They speak **G**erman.

5. Capitalize titles of works, such as books, movies, and pieces of art. If you look at the example paragraphs in this book, you will notice that each of them begins with a title. In a title, pay attention to which words begin with a capital letter and which words do not.

Gumbo	*A Lesson in Friendship*	*An Immigrant in the Family*
The King and I	*The Tale of Pinocchio*	*Love at First Sight*

   The rules for capitalizing titles are easy.

   - Always capitalize the first letter of a title.
   - If the title has more than one word, capitalize all the words that have meaning (content words).
   - Do not capitalize small (function) words, such as *a, an, and, the, in, with, on, for, to, above,* and *or.*

Capitalization Activities

Circle the words that have capitalization errors. Make the corrections above the errors.

1. the last day to sign up for the trip to sao paolo is this Thursday.

2. does jill live in west bay apartments, too?

3. the flight to Vancouver left late Saturday night and arrived early Sunday morning.

4. My sister has two daughters. Their names are rachel and rosalyn.

5. one of the most important sporting events is the world cup.

ACTIVITY 2

Complete these statements. Be sure to use correct capitalization.

1. *U.S.A.* stands for the United _____ of _____ .

2. The seventh month of the year is _____ .

3. _____ is the capital of Brazil.

4. One of the most popular brands of jeans is _____ .

5. The first person to walk on the moon was named _____ .

6. Parts of Europe were destroyed in _____ (1914–18).

7. My favorite restaurant is _____ .

8. Beijing is the largest city in _____ .

9. The winter months are _____ , _____ , and _____ .

10. The last movie that I saw was _____ .

ACTIVITY 3

Read the following titles. Rewrite them with correct capitalization.

1. my favorite food _____

2. living in montreal _____

3. the best restaurant in town _____

4. my best friend's new car _____

5. a new trend in Hollywood _____

6. why i left my country _____

7. my side of the mountain _____

8. no more room for a friend _____

ACTIVITY 4

Read the following paragraph. Circle the capitalization errors and make corrections above the errors.

Example Paragraph 2

A visit to Cuba

according to an article in last week's issue of *time*, the prime minister of canada will visit cuba soon in order to establish better economic ties between the two countries. because the united states does not have a history of good relations with cuba, canada's recent decision may result in problems between washington and ottawa. In an interview, the canadian prime minister indicated that his country was ready to reestablish some sort of cooperation with cuba and that canada would do so as quickly as possible. there is no doubt that this new development will be discussed at the opening session of congress next tuesday.

ACTIVITY 5

Read the following paragraph. Circle the capitalization errors and make corrections above the errors.

Example Paragraph 3

crossing the atlantic from atlanta

it used to be difficult to travel directly from atlanta to europe, but this is certainly not the case nowadays. union airways offers several daily flights to london. jetwings express offers flights every day to frankfurt and twice a week to berlin. other european air carriers that offer direct flights from atlanta to europe are valuair and luxliner. However, the airline with the largest number of direct flights to any european city is not a european airline. smead airlines, which is a new and rising airline in the united states, offers 17 flights a day to 12 european cities, including paris, london, frankfurt, zurich, rome, and athens.

Read the following paragraph. Circle the capitalization errors and make corrections above the errors.

Example Paragraph 4

my beginnings in foreign languages

I have always loved foreign languages. When I was in tenth grade, I took my first foreign language class. It was french I. My teacher was named mrs. montluzin. She was a wonderful teacher who inspired me to develop my interest in foreign languages. Before I finished high school, I took a second year of french and one year of spanish. I wish my high school had offered latin or greek, but the small size of the school body prevented this. Over the years since I graduated from high school, I have lived and worked abroad. I studied arabic when I lived in saudi arabia, japanese in japan, and malay in malaysia. Two years ago, I took a german class in the united states. Because of recent travels to uzbekistan and kyrgyzstan, which are two republics from the former soviet union, I have a strong desire to study russian. I hope that my love of learning foreign languages will continue.

Punctuation Activities
End Punctuation

The three most common punctuation marks found at the end of English sentences are the **period**, the **question mark**, and the **exclamation point**. It is important to know how to use all three of them correctly. Of these three, however, the period is by far the most commonly used punctuation mark.

1. **period** (.) A period is used at the end of a declarative sentence.

    This sentence is a declarative sentence.

    This sentence is not a question.

    All three of these sentences end with a period.

2. **question mark** (?) A question mark is used at the end of a question.

    Is this idea difficult?

    Is it hard to remember the name of this mark?

    How many questions are in this group?

3. **exclamation point** (!) An exclamation point is used at the end of an exclamation. It is less common than the other two marks.

> I cannot believe you think this topic is difficult!

> This is the best writing book in the world!

> Now I understand all of these examples!

ACTIVITY 1

Add the correct end punctuation.

1. Congratulations

2. Do most people think that the governor was unaware of the theft

3. Do not open your test booklet until you are told to do so

4. Will the president attend the meeting

5. Jason put the dishes in the dishwasher and then watched TV

ACTIVITY 2

Look at an article in any English newspaper or magazine. Circle every end punctuation mark. Then answer these questions.

1. How many final periods are there? _____ (or _____ %)

2. How many final question marks are there? _____ (or _____ %)

3. How many final exclamation points are there? _____ (or _____ %)

4. What is the total number of sentences? _____

Use this last number to calculate the percentages for each of the categories. Does the period occur most often?

Commas

The comma has several different functions in English. Here are some of the most common ones.

1. A comma separates a list of three or more things. There should be a comma between the items in a list.

> He speaks French and English. (No comma is needed because there are only two items.)

> She speaks French, English, and Chinese.

2. A comma separates two sentences when there is a combining word (coordinating conjunction) such as *and, but, or, so, for, nor,* and *yet.* The easy way to remember these conjunctions is *FANBOYS (for, and, nor, but, or, yet, so).*

> Six people took the course, but only five of them passed the test.

> Sammy bought the cake, and Paul paid for the ice cream.

> Students can register for classes in person, or they may submit their applications by mail.

3. A comma is used to separate an introductory word or phrase from the rest of the sentence.

> In conclusion, doctors are advising people to take more vitamins.

> First, you will need a pencil.

> Because of the heavy rains, many of the roads were flooded.

> Finally, add the nuts to the batter.

4. A comma is used to separate an appositive from the rest of the sentence. An appositive is a word or group of words that renames a noun before it. An appositive provides additional information about the noun.

subject (noun)　　　　　appositive　　　　　verb
Washington, the first president of the United States, was a clever military leader.

In this sentence, the phrase *the first president of the United States* is an appositive. This phrase renames or explains the noun *Washington*.

5. A comma is sometimes used with adjective clauses. An adjective clause usually begins with a relative pronoun *(who, that, which, whom, whose, whoever,* or *whomever)*. We use a comma when the information in the clause is unnecessary or extra. (This is also called a nonrestrictive clause.)

The book that is on the teacher's desk is the main book for this class.

(Here, when you say "the book," the reader does not know which book you are talking about, so the information in the adjective clause is necessary. In this case, do not set off the adjective clause with a comma.)

The History of Korea, which is on the teacher's desk, is the main book for this class.

(The name of the book is given, so the information in the adjective clause is not necessary to help the reader identify the book. In this case, you must use commas to show that the information in the adjective clause is extra, or nonrestrictive.)

ACTIVITY 3

Add commas as needed in these sentences. Some sentences may be correct, and others may need more than one comma.

1. For the past fifteen years Mary Parker has been both the director and producer of all the plays at this theater.

2. Despite all the problems we had on our vacation we managed to have a good time.

3. I believe the best countries to visit in Africa are Senegal Tunisia and Ghana.

4. She believes the best countries to visit in Africa are Senegal and Tunisia.

5. The third step in this process is to grate the carrots and the potatoes.

6. Third grate the carrots and the potatoes.

7. Blue green and red are strong colors. For this reason they are not appropriate for a living room wall.

8. Without anyone to teach foreign language classes next year the school will be unable to offer French Spanish or German.

9. The NEQ 7000 the very latest computer from Electron Technologies is not selling very well.

10. Because of injuries neither Carl nor Jamil two of the best players on the football team will be able to play in tomorrow's game.

11. The job interview is for a position at Mills Trust Company which is the largest company in this area.

12. The job interview is for a position at a large company that has more than 1,000 employees in this area.

13. Kevin's birthday is January 18 which is the same day that Laura and Greg have their birthdays.

14. Martina Navratilova whom most tennis fans refer to only as Martina dominated women's tennis for years.

15. My brother who lives in San Salvador has two children. (I have several brothers.)

16. My brother who lives in San Salvador has two children. (I have only one brother.)

17. This flight is leaving for La Paz which is the first of three stops that the plane will make.

18. No one knows the name of the person who will take over the committee in January so there have been many rumors about this.

19. Greenfield Central Bank the most recent bank to open a branch here in our area has tried to establish a branch here for years.

20. On the right side of the living room an antique radio sits on top of a glass table that also has a flowerpot a photo of a baby and a magazine.

Apostrophes

Apostrophes have two basic uses in English. They indicate either a contraction or possession.

Contractions: Use an apostrophe in a contraction in place of the letter or letters that have been deleted.

> He's (he is *or* he has), they're (they are), I've (I have), we'd (we would *or* we had)

Possession: Use an apostrophe to indicate possession. Add an apostrophe and the letter *s* after the word. If a plural word already ends in *s*, then just add an apostrophe.

> Gandhi's role in the history of India
> Yesterday's paper
> the boy's books (One boy has some books.)
> the boys' books (Several boys have one or more books.)

ACTIVITY 4

Correct the apostrophe errors in these sentences.

1. I am going to Victors birthday party on Saturday.

2. My three cousins house is right next to Mr. Wilsons house.

3. Hardly anyone remembers Stalins drastic actions in the early part of the last century.

4. It goes without saying that wed be better off without so much poverty in this world.

5. The reasons that were given for the childrens bad behavior were unbelievable.

Quotation Marks

Below are three of the most common uses for quotation marks.

1. To mark the exact words that were spoken by someone:

   The king said, "I refuse to give up my throne." (The period is inside the quotation marks.)*

   "None of the solutions is correct," said the professor. (The comma is inside the quotation marks.)*

   The king said that he refuses to give up his throne. (No quotation marks are needed because the sentence does not include the king's exact words. This style is called indirect speech.)

   * Note that the comma separates the verb that tells the form of communications (*said, announced, wrote*) and the quotation.

2. To mark language that a writer has borrowed from another source:

   The dictionary defines gossip as an "informal conversation, often about other people's private affairs," but I would add that it is usually malicious.

   This research concludes that there was "no real reason to expect this computer software program to produce good results with high school students."

   According to an article in *The San Jose Times,* about half of the money was stolen. (No quotes are necessary here because it is a summary of information rather than exact words from the article.)

3. To indicate when a word or phrase is being used in a special way:

   The king believed himself to be the leader of a democracy, so he allowed the prisoner to choose his method of dying. According to the king, allowing this kind of "democracy" showed that he was indeed a good ruler.

ACTIVITY 5

Add quotation marks where necessary. Remember the rules for placing commas, periods, and question marks inside or outside the quotation marks.

1. As I was leaving the room, I heard the teacher say, Be sure to study Chapter 7.

2. It is impossible to say that using dictionaries is useless. However, according to research published in the latest issue of the *General Language Journal,* dictionary use is down. I found the article's statement that 18.3 percent of students do not own a dictionary and 37.2 percent never use their dictionary (p. 75) to be rather shocking.

   Source: Wendt, John "Dictionary Use by Language Students," *General Language Journal* 3 (2007): 72-101.

3. My fiancée says that if I buy her a huge diamond ring, this would be a sign that I love her. I would like to know if there is a less expensive sign that would be a sure sign of my love for her.

4. When my English friend speaks of a heat wave just because the temperature reaches over 80°, I have to laugh because I come from Thailand, where we have sunshine most of the year. The days when we have to dress warmly are certainly few, and some people wear shorts outside almost every month of the year.

5. The directions on the package read, Open carefully. Add contents to one glass of warm water. Drink just before bedtime.

Semicolons

The semicolon is used most often to combine two related sentences. Once you get used to using the semicolon, you will find that it is a very easy and useful punctuation tool to vary the sentences in your writing.

- Use a semicolon when you want to connect two simple sentences.

- The function of a semicolon is similar to that of a period. However, in order to use a semicolon, there must be a relationship between the sentences.

> Joey loves to play tennis. He has been playing since he was ten years old.

> Joey loves to play tennis; he has been playing since he was ten years old.

Both sentence pairs are correct. The main difference is that the semicolon in the second example signals the relationship between the ideas in the two sentences. Notice also that *he* is not capitalized in the second example.

ACTIVITY 6

The following sentences use periods for separation. Rewrite the sentences. Replace the periods with semicolons and make any other necessary changes.

1. Gretchen and Bob have been friends since elementary school. They are also next-door neighbors.

_____

2. The test was complicated. No one passed it.

_____

3. Tomatoes are necessary for a garden salad. Peas are not.

_____

4. Mexico lies to the south of the United States. Canada lies to the north.

_____

Look at a copy of an English newspaper or magazine. Circle all the semicolons on a page. The number should be relatively small.

NOTE: If the topic of the article is technical or complex, there is a greater chance of finding semicolons. Semicolons are not usually used in informal or friendly writing. Thus, you might see a semicolon in an article about heart surgery or educational research, but not in an ad for a household product or an e-mail or text message to a friend.

Editing for Errors

ACTIVITY 8

Find the 14 punctuation errors in this paragraph and make corrections above the errors.

Example Paragraph 5

An Unexpected Storm

Severe weather is a constant possibility all over the globe; but we never really expect our own area to be affected However last night was different At about ten o'clock a tornado hit Lucedale This violent weather destroyed nine homes near the downtown area In addition to these nine houses that were completely destroyed many others in the area had heavy damage Amazingly no one was injured in last nights terrible storm Because of the rapid reaction of state and local weather watchers most of the areas residents saw the warnings that were broadcast on television

ACTIVITY 9

Find the 15 punctuation errors in this paragraph and make corrections above the errors.

Example Paragraph 6

Deserts

Deserts are some of the most interesting places on earth A desert is not just a dry area it is an area that receives less than ten inches of rainfall a year About one-fifth of the earth is composed of deserts Although many people believe that deserts are nothing but hills of sand this is not true In reality deserts have large rocks mountains canyons and even lakes For instance only about ten percent of the Sahara Desert the largest desert on the earth is sand

Find the 15 punctuation errors in this paragraph and make corrections above the errors.

A Review

    I Wish I Could Have Seen His Face Marilyn Kings latest novel is perhaps her greatest triumph In this book King tells the story of the Lamberts a poor family that struggles to survive despite numerous hardships. The Lambert family consists of five strong personalities. Michael Lambert has trouble keeping a job and Naomi earns very little as a maid at a hotel The three children range in age from nine to sixteen. Dan Melinda and Zeke are still in school This well-written novel allows us to step into the conflict that each of the children has to deal with. Only a writer as talented as King could develop five independent characters in such an outstanding manner The plot has many unexpected turns and the outcome of this story will not disappoint readers While King has written several novels that won international praise *I Wish I Could Have Seen His Face* is in many ways better than any of her previous works.

Additional Grammar Activities
Verb Tense

Fill in the blanks with the verb that best completes the sentence. Be sure to use the correct form of the verb. Use the following verbs: *like, cut, break, stir,* and *spread.*

A Simple Sandwich

    Making a tuna salad sandwich is not difficult. Put two cans of flaked tuna in a medium-sized bowl. With a fork, _____ the fish apart. _____ up a large white onion or two small yellow onions. _____ in one-third cup of mayonnaise. Then

add salt and pepper to taste. Some people _____ to mix
pieces of boiled eggs into their salad. Once you finish making the salad,

_____ it between two slices of bread. Now you are ready to
eat your easy-to-make treat.

ACTIVITY 2
Fill in the blanks with the correct form of any appropriate verb.

Example Paragraph 9

Who Killed Kennedy?

One of the most infamous moments in U.S. history _____
in 1963. In that year, President John F. Kennedy _____
assassinated in Dallas, Texas. Since this event, there _____
many theories about what _____ on that fateful day.
According to the official U.S. government report, only one man

_____ the bullets that _____ President
Kennedy. However, even today many people _____ that
there _____ several assassins.

ACTIVITY 3
Fill in the blanks with the correct form of any appropriate verb.

Example Paragraph 10

A Routine Routine

I have one of the most boring daily routines of anyone I

_____ . Every morning, I _____ at 7:15.1
_____ a shower and _____ dressed.
After that, I _____ breakfast and _____
to the office. I _____ from 8:30 to 4:30. Then I
_____ home. This _____ five days a week
without fail. Just for once, I wish something different would happen!

Fill in the blanks with the correct form of the verbs in parentheses.

Example Paragraph 11

The Shortest Term in the White House

William Henry Harrison (be) _____ the ninth
president of the United States. His presidency was extremely brief.
In fact, Harrison (be) _____ president for only one
month. He (take) _____ office on March 4,1841.
Unfortunately he (catch) _____ a cold that (become)
_____ pneumonia. On April 4, Harrison (die)
_____ . He (become) _____ the first
American president to die while in office. Before becoming president,
Harrison (study) _____ to become a doctor and later
(serve) _____ in the army.

ACTIVITY 5

Fill in the blanks with the correct form of the verbs in parentheses.

Example Paragraph 12

The History of Brownsville

Brownsville, Texas, is a city with an interesting history. Brownsville
(be) _____ originally a fort during the Mexican-
American War. During that war, American and Mexican soldiers (fight)
_____ several battles in the area around the city. As a
matter of fact, the city (get) _____ its name from Major
Jacob Brown, an American soldier who was killed in a battle near the
old fort. However, Brownsville's history (be) _____
not only connected to war. After the war, the city was best known for
farming. The area's rich soil (help) _____ it become
a thriving agriculture center. Over time, the agricultural industry
(grow) _____ , and today Brownsville farmers (be)
_____ well-known for growing cotton and citrus. In sum,
both the Mexican-American War and farming have played important
historical roles in making Brownsville such an interesting city.

Articles

ACTIVITY 6

Fill in the blanks with the correct article. If no article is required, write an X in the blank.

Example Paragraph 13

_____ Simple Math Problem

There is _____ interesting mathematics brainteaser that always amazes _____ people when they first hear it. First, pick _____ number from _____ 1 to _____ 9. Subtract _____ 5. (You may have a negative number.) Multiply this answer by _____ 3. Now square _____ number. Then add _____ digits of _____ number. For _____ example, if your number is 81, add 8 and 1 to get an answer of _____ 9. If _____ number is less than _____ 5, add _____ 5. If _____ number is not less than _____ 5, subtract _____ 4. Now multiply this number by _____ 2. Finally, subtract _____ 6. If you have followed _____ steps correctly, _____ your answer is _____ 4.

ACTIVITY 7

Fill in the blanks with the correct article. If no article is required, write an X in the blank.

Example Paragraph 14

_____ Geography Problems among _____ American Students

Are _____ American high school students _____ less educated in _____ geography than high school students in _____ other countries? According to _____ recent survey of _____ high school students all over _____ globe, _____ U.S. students do not know very much about _____ geography. For _____ example, _____ surprisingly large number did not know _____ capital of _____ state in which they live. Many could not find _____ Mexico on a map even though Mexico is one of _____ two countries that share _____ border with _____ United States. Some _____ educators blame this lack of _____ geographical knowledge on the move away from memorization of material that has taken _____ place in _____ recent years in American schools. Regardless of _____ cause, the unfortunate fact appears to be that American _____ high school students are not learning enough about this subject area.

Fill in the blanks with the correct article. If no article is required, write an X in the blank.

Example Paragraph 15

_____ Homeowners Saving _____ Money with a New Free Service

People who are concerned that their monthly electricity bill is too high can now take _____ advantage of _____ special free service offered by the local electricity company. _____ company will do _____ home energy audit on any house to find out if _____ house is wasting _____ valuable energy. Homeowners can call _____ power company to schedule _____ convenient time for _____ energy analyst to visit their home. The audit takes only about _____ hour. _____ analyst will inspect _____ home and identify potential energy-saving _____ improvements. For _____ example, he or she will check _____ thermostat, the air-conditioning, and _____ seals around doors and windows. The major energy-use _____ problems will be identified, and _____ analyst will recommend _____ ways to use _____ energy more efficiently.

Fill in the blanks with the correct article. If no article is required, write an X in the blank.

Example Paragraph 16

_____ **Great Teacher**

To this day, I am completely convinced that _____ main reason that I did so well in my French class in _____ high school was the incredible teacher that I had, _____ Mrs. Montluzin. I had not studied _____ foreign language before I started _____ Mrs. Montluzin's French class. _____ idea of being able to communicate in a foreign language, especially _____ French, intrigued me, but _____ idea also scared me. _____ French seemed so difficult at first. We had so much _____ vocabulary to memorize, and we had to do _____ exercises to improve our grammar. While it is true that there was _____ great deal of work to do, _____ Mrs. Montluzin always tried her best to make French class very interesting. She also gave us _____ suggestions for learning _____ French, and these helped me a lot. Since this French class, I have studied a few other languages, and my interest in _____ foreign languages today is due to _____ success I had in French class with _____ Mrs. Montluzin.

ACTIVITY 10

Fill in the blanks with the correct article. If no article is required, write an X in the blank.

Example Paragraph 17

_____ **Surprising Statistics on** _____ **Higher Education in** _____ **United States**

Although _____ United States is a leader in many areas, it is surprising that _____ number of Americans with _____ college degree is not as high as it is in some _____ other countries. Only about 22 percent of

_____ Americans have attended college for four or more

years. To _____ most people, this rather low ratio of one

in five is shocking. Slightly more than _____ 60 percent

of _____ Americans between _____

ages of 25 and 40 have taken some _____ college classes.

Though these numbers are far from what _____ many

people would expect in _____ United States, these

statistics are _____ huge improvement over figures

at _____ turn of _____ last century.

In _____ 1900, only about _____ 8

percent of all Americans even entered _____ college. At

_____ present time, there are about 21 million students

attending _____ college.

Editing for Errors

ACTIVITY 11

This paragraph contains eight errors. They are in word choice (one), article (one), modal* (one), verb tense (one), subject-verb agreement (three), and word order (one). Mark these errors and write the corrections above the errors.

Example Paragraph 18

A Dangerous Driving Problem

Imagine that you are driving your car home from mall or the library. You come to a bend in the road. You decide that you need to slow down a little, so you tap the brake pedal. Much to your surprise, the car does not begin to slow down. You push the brake pedal all the way down to the floor, but still anything happens. There are a few things you can do when your brakes does not work. One was to pump the brakes. If also this fails, you should to try the emergency brake. If this also fail, you should try to shift the car into a lower gear and rub the tires against the curb until the car come to a stop.

*Modals are *can, should, will, must, may,* and *might.* Modals appear before verbs. We do not use *to* between modals and verbs. (*Incorrect:* I should to go with him. *Correct:* I should go with him.) Modals do not have forms that take *-s, -ing,* or *-ed.*

This paragraph contains ten errors. They are in prepositions (three), word order (one), articles (two), and verb tense (four). Mark these errors and write the corrections above the errors.

Example Paragraph 19

The Start of My Love of Aquariums

My love of aquariums began a long time ago. Although I got my first fish when I am just seven years old, I can still remember the store, the fish, and salesclerk who waited on me that day. Because I made good grades on my report card, my uncle has rewarded me with a dollar. A few days later, I was finally able to go to the local dime store for spend my money. It was 1965, and dollar could buy a lot. I looked a lot of different things, but I finally chose to buy a fish. We had an old fishbowl at home, so it seems logical with me to get a fish. I must have spent 15 minutes pacing back and forth in front of all the aquariums before I finally choose my fish. It was a green swordtail, or rather, she was a green swordtail. A few weeks later, she gave birth to 20 or 30 baby swordtails. Years later, I can still remember the fish beautiful that got me so interested in aquariums.

ACTIVITY 13

This paragraph contains eight errors. They are in prepositions (one), articles (three), word forms (two), verb tense (one), and subject-verb agreement (one). Mark these errors and write the corrections above the errors.

Example Paragraph 20

An Effect of Cellphones on Drivers

Cellular phones, can be threat to safety. A recent study for Donald Redelmeier and Robert Tibshirani of the University of Toronto showed that cellular phones pose a risk to drivers. In fact, people who talk on the phone while driving are four time more likely to have an automobile accident than those who do not use the phone while drive. The Toronto researchers studied 699 drivers who had been in an automobile accident while they were using their cellular phones. The researchers concluded that the main reason for the accidents is not that people used one hand for the telephone and only one for driving. Rather, cause of the accidents was usually that the drivers became distracted, angry, or upset by the phone call. The drivers then lost concentration and was more prone to a car accident.

This paragraph contains seven errors. They are in verb tense (one), articles (two), word forms (three), and subject-verb agreement (one). Mark these errors and write the corrections.

Example Paragraph 21

Problems with American Coins

Many foreigners who come to the United States have very hard time getting used to America coins. The denominations of the coins are one, five, ten, 25, and 50 cents, and one dollar. However, people used only the first four regularly. The smallest coin in value is the penny, but it is not the smallest coin in size. The quarter is one-fourth the value of a dollar, but it is not one-fourth as big as a dollar. There is a dollar coin, but no one ever use it. In fact, perhaps the only place to find one is at a bank. All of the coins are silver-colored except for one, the penny. Finally, because value of each coin is not clearly written on the coin as it is in many country, foreigners often experience problems with monetarily transactions.

ACTIVITY 15

This paragraph contains seven errors. They are in word order (one), articles (two), preposition (one), subject-verb agreement (one), and verb tense (two). Mark these errors and write the corrections.

Example Paragraph 22

An Oasis of Silence

Life on this campus can be extremely hectic, so when I want the solitude, I go usually to the fourth floor of the library. The fourth floor has nothing but shelves and shelves of rare books and obscure periodicals. Because there are only a few small tables with some rather uncomfortable wooden chairs and no copy machines in this floor, few people are staying here very long. Students search for a book or periodical, found it, and then take it to a more sociable floor to photocopy the pages or simply browse through the articles. One of my best friends have told me that he does not like this floor that is so special to me. For him, it is a lonely place. For me, however, it is oasis of silence in a land of turmoil, a place where I can read, think, and write in peace.

Useful Vocabulary for Better Writing

These useful words and phrases can help you write better sentences and paragraphs. They can make your writing sound more academic, natural, and fluent.

Giving and Adding Examples

Words and Phrases	Examples
For example, S + V / *For instance,* S + V	Our reading teacher assigns a lot of homework. *For example,* last night we had to read ten pages and write an essay.
The first reason + VERB	The article we read in class gave three reasons that our planet is in trouble. *The first reason* is about the increasing population.

Concluding Sentences

Words and Phrases	Examples
In conclusion, S + V	*In conclusion,* I believe everyone should vote in every election.
By doing all of these things, S + V	*By doing all of these things,* we can improve education in our country.
Because of this, S + V	*Because of this,* many people will have better health care.
As a result, S + V	*As a result,* I chose to go to college in France instead of my country.
For these reasons, S + V	*For these reasons,* I prefer to eat at home instead of a restaurant.
In sum, S + V / *In summary,* S + V / *To summarize ,* S + V	*In sum,* World War II was a very complicated war with many countries fighting for very different reasons, but in many ways, it was a continuation of World War I.
In other words, S + V	*In other words,* the judge made an incorrect decision.
From the information given, we can conclude that S + V	*From the information given, we can conclude that* Mark Johnson is certainly the best soccer player in this decade.
It is clear that S + V	*It is clear that* exercising every day improved your health.

Comparing

Words and Phrases	Examples
NOUN *is* COMPARATIVE ADJECTIVE *than* NOUN	New York *is larger than* Rhode Island.
S + V + COMPARATIVE ADVERB *than* Y.	The cats ran *faster than* the dogs.
S + V. *In comparison,* S + V.	Canada has provinces. *In comparison,* Brazil has states.
Although NOUN *and* NOUN *are similar in* NOUN, S + V	*Although* France *and* Spain *are similar in* size, they are different in many ways.
NOUN *and* NOUN *are similar.*	Brazil *and* the United States *are* surprisingly *similar.*
NOUN *is the same*	Our house *is the same* size as your house.
…as ADJECTIVE *as…*	Our house is *as big as* your house.
Like NOUN, NOUN *also*	*Like* Brazil, Mexico *also* has states.
both NOUN *and* NOUN*…*	In *both* German *and* Japanese, the verb appears at the end of a sentence.

Likewise, S + V / Also, S + V	The blooms on the red roses last longer than most other flowers. *Likewise*, the blooms for the pink rose are long-lasting.
Similarly, S + V .../ *Similar to* NOUN	Economists believe India has a bright future. *Similarly*, Brazil's future is on a very positive track.

Contrasting

Words and Phrases	Examples
S + V. *In contrast*, S + V.	*Algeria* is a very large country. *In contrast*, the UAE is very small.
Contrasted with / *In contrast to* NOUN	*In contrast to* last year, our company has doubled its profits this year.
Although / *Even though* / *Though* S + V	*Although* Spain and France are similar in size, they are different in many other ways.
Unlike NOUN,	*Unlike* the pink roses, the red roses are very expensive.
However, S + V	Canada has provinces. *However*, Brazil has states.
On the one hand, S + V *On the other hand*, S + V	*On the one hand*, Maggie loved to travel. *On the other hand*, she hated to be away from her home.
The opposite S + V	Most of the small towns in my state are experiencing a boom in tourism. In my hometown, *the opposite* is true.
NOUN *and* NOUN *are different.*	My older brother *and* my younger brother *are very different.*

Telling a Story / Narrating

Words and Phrases	Examples
When I was X, I would VERB	*When I was* a child, *I would* go fishing every weekend.
I have never felt so ADJ *in my life.*	*I have never felt so* anxious *in my life.*
I will never forget NOUN	*I will never forget* the day I took my first international flight.
I can still remember NOUN / *I will always remember* NOUN	*I can still remember* the day I started my first job.
NOUN *was the best / worst day of my life.*	My wedding was *the best day of my life.*
Every time X happened, Y happened.	*Every time* I used that computer, I had a problem.
This was my first ...	*This was my first* job after graduating from college.

Describing a Process

Words and Phrases	Examples
First (Second, Third, etc.), ... *Next,... After that,...Then,...* *Finally,...*	*First*, I cut the apples into small pieces. *Next*, I added some mayonnaise. *After that*, I added some salt. *Finally*, I mixed everything together well.
The first thing you should do is VERB	*The first thing you should do is* turn on the computer.
VERB+-*ing requires you to follow (number) of steps.*	*Saving* a file on a computer *requires you to follow several simple steps.*
Before you VERB, *you should* VERB.	*Before you* write a paragraph, *you should* brainstorm for ideas.
After (When)...	*After* you brainstorm your ideas, you can select the best ones to write about in your essay.

After that, …	After that, you can select the best ones to write about in your essay.
The last step is… / Finally, …	Finally, you should cook all of the ingredients for an hour.
If you follow these important steps in VERB + -ing,…	If you follow these important steps in applying for a passport, you will have your new document in a very short time.

Defining

Words and Phrases	Examples
The NOUN, which is a/an NOUN + ADJECTIVE CLAUSE, MAIN VERB	An owl, which is a bird that has huge round eyes, is awake most of the night.
According to the dictionary…	According to The Collins Cobuild Dictionary of American English, gossip is "an informal conversation, often about people's private affairs."
The dictionary definition of NOUN	The dictionary definition of gumbo is not very good.
X released a report stating that S + V	The president's office released a report stating that the new law will require all adults between the ages of 18 and 30 to serve at least one year of active military duty.
In other words, S + V	In other words, we have to redo everything we have done so far.
,…which means…	The paper is due tomorrow, which means if you want to get a good grade, you need to finish it today.
NOUN means…	Gossip means talking or writing about other people's private affairs.

Showing Cause and Effect

Words and Phrases	Examples
Because of NOUN, S + V. Because S + V, S + V.	Because of the traffic problems, it is easy to see why the city is building a new tunnel.
NOUN can trigger NOUN. NOUN can cause NOUN.	An earthquake can trigger tidal waves and can cause massive destruction.
Due to NOUN, …	Due to the snowstorm, all schools will be closed tomorrow.
As a result of NOUN…	As a result of his efforts, he got a better job.
Therefore,…/ As a result,…/ For this reason,…/ Consequently,…	It suddenly began to rain. Therefore, we all got wet.
NOUN will bring about …	The use of the Internet will bring about a change in education.
NOUN has had a good / bad effect on…	Computer technology has had both positive and negative effects on society.
The correlation is clear / evident.	The correlation between junk food and obesity is clear.

Describing

Words and Phrases	Examples
Prepositions of location: *above, across, around, in the dark, near, under…*	The children raced their bikes *around* the school.
Descriptive adjectives: *wonderful, delightful, dangerous, informative, rusty…*	The *bent, rusty* bike squeaked when I rode it.
SUBJECT *is* ADJECTIVE.	This dictionary *is informative*.
X is the most ADJECTIVE + NOUN.	To me, Germany *is the most interesting* country in Europe.
X tastes / looks / smells / feels like NOUN.	My ID card *looks like* a credit card.
X is known / famous for its NOUN.	France *is known for* its cheese.

Stating an Opinion

Words and Phrases	Examples
Without a doubt, VERB *is* ADJECTIVE *idea / method / decision / way.*	*Without a doubt,* walking to work each day *is* an excellent *way* to lose weight.
Personally, I believe/think/feel/agree/ disagree/ suppose S + V.	*Personally, I believe that* smoking on a bus should not be allowed.
VERB+-*ing should not be allowed.*	Smoking in public *should not be allowed.*
In my opinion/ view/ experience, NOUN	*In my opinion,* smoking is rude.
For this reason, S + V. / *That is why I think…*	I do not have a car. *For this reason,* I do not care about rising gasoline prices.
There are many benefits / advantages to NOUN.	*There are many benefits* to swimming every day.
There are many drawbacks / disadvantages to NOUN.	*There are many drawbacks* to eating your meals at a restaurant.
I am convinced that S + V	*I am convinced that* education at a university should be free to all citizens.
NOUN *should be required / mandatory.*	College *should be required.*
I prefer NOUN *to* NOUN.	*I prefer* soccer to football.
To me, banning / prohibiting NOUN *makes (perfect) sense.*	*To me, banning* cell phones while driving *makes perfect sense.*
For all of these important reasons, I think / believe / feel (that) S + V	*For all of these important reasons, I think* smoking *should be* banned in public.
Based on X, I have come to the conclusion that S + V	*Based on* two books that I read recently, *I have come to the conclusion that* global warming is the most serious problem that my generation faces.

Arguing and Persuading

Words and Phrases	Examples
It is important to remember that S + V	*It is important to remember* that school uniforms would only be worn during school hours.
According to a recent survey, S + V	*According to a recent survey,* 85 percent of high school students felt they had too much homework.
Even more important, S + V	*Even more important,* statistics show the positive effects that school uniforms have on behavior.
Despite this, S + V	The report says this particular kind of airplane is dangerous. *Despite this,* the government has not banned this airplane.
SUBJECT *must / should / ought to* VERB	Researchers *must* stop unethical animal testing.
The reason for S + V	*The reason for* people's support of this plan is that it provides equal treatment for all citizens.
To emphasize, S + V	*To emphasize,* I support a lower age for voting but only for those who already have a high school diploma.
For these reasons, S + V	*For these reasons,* public schools should require uniforms.
Obviously, S + V	*Obviously,* there are many people who would disagree with what I have just said.
Without a doubt, S + V	*Without a doubt,* students ought to learn a foreign language.
I agree that S + V. *However* S + V	*I agree that* a college degree is important. *However,* getting a practical technical license can also be very useful.

Reacting/Responding

Words and Phrases	Examples
TITLE *by* AUTHOR *is a / an...*	*Harry Potter and the Goblet of Fire* by J.K. Rowling *is an* entertaining book to read.
My first reaction to the prompt / news / article was / is NOUN.	*My first reaction to the article was* fear.
When I read / look at / think about NOUN, *I was amazed / shocked / surprised ...*	*When I read* the article, *I was surprised* to learn of his athletic ability.